YOUTH WORSHIP
SOURCE BOOK
Sarah Kathleen Johnson

Youth Worship Source Book
By Sarah Kathleen Johnson

Copyright © 2009 by Faith & Life Resources, a division of Mennonite Publishing Network, Scottdale, PA 15683 and Waterloo, ON N2L 6H7

Unless otherwise noted, Scripture text is quoted, with permission, from the New Revised Standard Version, © 1989, Division of Christian Education of the National Council of Churches of Christ in the United States of America.

International Standard Book Number: 978-0-8361-9470-8

Design by Reuben Graham

Printed in the United States of America

Orders and information
USA: 800-245-7894
Canada: 800-631-6535
www.mpn.net

Introduction 5

Unit 1: Introduction to Worship 8

Content for Teaching and Learning 8

Curriculum Modules
Module 1: Worship: Where, Who, What, Why, and When? 13
Module 2: The Role of the Worship Leader and Speaking Words in Worship 17
Module 3: Thematic Worship and the Christian Year 21

Unit 2: Opening and Closing Worship 25

Content for Teaching and Learning 25

Curriculum Modules
Module 1: Opening and Closing Worship 28
Module 2: Worship Language and Finding Words for Worship 32
Module 3: Writing Opening and Closing Words Together 37

Youth Worship Leadership Suggestions 42

Unit 3: Music in Worship **44**

Content for Teaching and Learning 45

Curriculum Modules
Module 1: Appreciating Diversity 47
Module 2: The Words We Sing 50
Module 3: The Music We Sing 54
Module 4: Choosing Music for Worship 59

Youth Worship Leadership Suggestions 62

Unit 4: Prayer **63**

Content for Teaching and Learning 64

Curriculum Modules
Module 1: Introduction to Prayer in Worship 68
Module 2: The Creative Process 72
Module 3: Leading Prayer Together 76

Youth Worship Leadership Suggestions 79

Unit 5: Visuals **80**

Content for Teaching and Learning 81

Curriculum Modules
Module 1: Imaging Worship 85
Module 2: Images in Worship 89
Module 3: Designing Images for Worship 93

Youth Worship Leadership Suggestions 97

Unit 6: Scripture **98**

Content for Teaching and Learning 99

Curriculum Modules
    Module 1: Introduction to Scripture in Worship 102
    Module 2: Reading and Listening to Scripture in Worship 107
    Module 3: Creatively Presenting Scripture in Worship Together 112

Youth Worship Leadership Suggestions 114

Unit 7: Preaching **115**

Content for Teaching and Learning 116

Curriculum Modules
    Module 1: Introduction to Preaching 120
    Module 2: Listening and Responding to Preaching 123
    Module 3: Preaching Together 126

Youth Worship Leadership Suggestions 131

Unit 8: The Body and the Senses **132**

Content for Teaching and Learning 132

Curriculum Modules
    Module 1: Movement in Worship 134
    Module 2: Planning Multisensory Worship Together 138

Youth Worship Leadership Suggestions 142

Unit 9: Offering **144**

Content for Teaching and Learning 144

Curriculum Modules
    Module 1: The Budget 147
    Module 2: Personal Giving 151
    Module 3: Offering as Worship 154

Youth Worship Leadership Suggestions 157

Unit 10: The Lord's Supper **159**

Content for Teaching and Learning 159

Curriculum Modules
    Module 1: Introduction to the Lord's Supper 162
    Module 2: Baking Bread Together 168

Youth Worship Leadership Suggestions 170

Appendix 1: Youth Worship Service Planning Guide **171**

Appendix 2: Worship Leadership Gifts Survey **173**

Acknowledgments **175**

Youth Worship Source Book

Introduction

Why invite youth to plan and lead worship?

Youth worship leadership integrates youth into the life of the church. It makes it clear worship is a place where they are welcome and belong. It identifies and nourishes leadership skills that allow youth to contribute to church in the present and the future. Integrating youth into worship leadership gives them a deeper understanding of worship. It develops skills that enable them to participate more fully in worship

Youth add energy and creativity to worship. They can challenge the congregation to worship in a way that reflects the diverse experiences and gifts of the entire community of faith, including young people. Youth worship leadership forges connections between the youth program and the Sunday service, encouraging participation in both aspects of church life.

What does *Source Book* do?

Source Book is designed to:
- Create space for youth to reflect on and discuss worship.
- Equip youth with the skills and confidence to plan and lead worship.
- Provide opportunities for youth to apply their knowledge in leading elements of the Sunday service.

What is included in *Source Book*?

Source Book is composed of units that address different aspects of worship. A youth worship service planning guide is included in *Appendix 1* (p. 171) and a gift discernment questionnaire in *Appendix 2* (p. 173).

What is included in each unit?

Content for Learning and Teaching—a summary of the topics addressed in the unit and a list of additional resources. For more resources, contact members of your congregation or your local area conference.

Curriculum Modules—two to four 45-minute curriculum modules that teach the foundational concepts in the chapter. The modules provide a framework for leading the portion of the service addressed in each unit.

Youth Worship Leadership Suggestions (in all units except Unit 1)—a list of practical suggestions and creative ideas for youth to lead an element of a Sunday morning worship service related to the unit topic. A youth worship leadership checklist is also included.

What is included in each curriculum module?

Opening activity—creates a space for discussion or worship preparation. The activity can range from a game to a time of prayer. Options are given for incorporating youth who do not arrive at the beginning of the module. Adaptations for small and large groups, as well as different energy levels, are also provided.

Discussion or preparation for worship—the core of the module includes discussion, creative presentation of information, or preparing to lead worship. Discussion is often effective in smaller groups of three to five youth. With a larger group, consider dividing into small discussion groups and reuniting to share ideas.

Reflection and prayer—the conclusion of each module. Worship is not confined to Sunday morning, but is part of daily life. It is essential for worship leaders to practice spiritual disciplines and grow as people of faith. Move to a new space, use a consistent visual focus, and develop a clear auditory signal to focus the attention of the group and define the beginning and end of quiet reflection. For example, sit around a cross, candle, or alternative symbol, and start and finish with a rainstick, singing bowl, or gong. Music suggestions are provided for some modules, but use music that is meaningful in your context. Incorporate a wide range of styles, borrowing from religious and secular sources. Use instrumental music if you cannot find music with relevant lyrics. Consider live music provided by youth leaders or youth. Do not be afraid of silence. Even the most energetic group can learn to be quiet together.

Teaching moment—indicates information the group needs to know. You don't have to read the material exactly as it is written. Feel free to state it in a way that is clear to your group.

What are the underlying goals of each module?
- Talk about and plan worship in a way that is fun and engaging.
- Foster discussion about worship among all participants.
- Challenge youth of a diverse range of personality types and learning styles to find their place in worship and worship leadership.
- Provide worship education and leadership activities that can be adapted for a variety of worship settings, styles, and themes, as well as youth group sizes, interests, and abilities.
- Offer a framework for creative worship planning and leadership with space for tradition and new contributions. There are no bad ideas, only ideas that require adaptation.
- Encourage the youth to reflect on what it means to worship and lead in worship, without suggesting a "right" or "wrong" way to worship.

How do I use *Source Book*?
Each unit includes curriculum modules for teaching about worship and preparing to lead worship. The units and modules in this book are like Scrabble™ tiles. You can select and rearrange combinations of units and modules to create elements of worship suitable for diverse worship settings and the particular gifts and interests of the youth. Freely and creatively adapt and rearrange the material.

In the introduction to each unit, different combinations of modules are recommended for various purposes and time frames. Modules can also be combined across units. Two survey options are outlined below. For a focus on worship education, youth are introduced to each topic, but not given opportunities for worship leadership. The worship leadership focus helps youth plan and lead worship.

Worship Education Focus	*Worship Leadership Focus*
Unit 1 Modules 1 and 3	Unit 1 Module 2
Unit 2 Module 1	Unit 2 Modules 2 and 3
Unit 3 Modules 1 and 3	Unit 3 Modules 2 and 4
Unit 4 Module 1	Unit 4 Modules 2 and 3
Unit 5 Modules 1 and 2	Unit 5 Module 3
Unit 6 Module 1	Unit 6 Modules 2 and 3
Unit 7 Modules 1 and 2	Unit 7 Module 3
Unit 8 Module 1	Unit 8 Module 2
Unit 9 Modules 1 and 2	Unit 9 Modules 3 and 4
Unit 10 Module 1	Unit 10 Module 2

How do I successfully integrate youth into worship planning and leadership?

- *Collaborate.* Draw on the resources available within your congregation. Contact individuals involved in worship leadership. Work together to determine themes and Scripture texts, and find appropriate times and ways for youth to be involved.
- *Communicate.* Ensure that youth, parents, and other worship leaders are fully informed. Provide a list of dates the group will be involved in worship weeks or months in advance.
- *Be clear and flexible.* Make clear and detailed plans but be prepared to adapt. Things will change at the last minute.
- *Involve individuals.* Invite and support individual youth with particular gifts and interests to lead aspects of worship in addition to leading worship as a group.
- *Pray.* Listen and speak to God on your own, with the youth, and as a congregation.

Before you start using this sourcebook . . .

Consider these youth worship leadership suggestions

- Plan and lead aspects of worship on a regular basis, using the curriculum modules in *Youth Worship Source Book.*
- Plan and lead an annual service in which every aspect of worship is prepared and facilitated by the youth. See the Youth Service Guide in Appendix 1.
- Involve individuals or small groups of youth in worship leadership according to their personal gifts and abilities. See the Gift Discernment Questionnaire in Appendix 2.
- Invite one or more youth to serve on a seasonal or congregational worship planning committee.
- Invite one or more youth to help plan a special service, such as a service for Christmas Eve, Good Friday, or a church picnic.
- Create mentoring relationships that pair youth interested in worship planning and leadership with experienced worship planners and leaders.
- Evaluate current worship structures with the youth, inviting them to reflect on what helps them worship and what hinders them. Pass their suggestions on to the pastor or worship planning committee.

Youth Worship Leadership Checklist

Spiritual:
1. Are youth given opportunities to share their gifts and spiritual experiences with the congregation in worship leadership, as individuals and as a group?
2. Is the congregation encouraged to gratefully receive the gifts offered by the youth in worship leadership?
3. Are youth encouraged to deepen their personal relationships with God?

Logistical:
1. Is there clear communication between youth leaders and worship leaders?

What Is Worship?

Unit focus

Worship is at the centre of who the church is and what the church does. There are as many different forms of worship as there are church communities. This unit explores the question, "What is worship?" as well as the role of the Christian year in shaping worship and the nature of worship leadership.

This unit does not offer guidelines for a specific youth leadership role in the Sunday service. Module 1 can be used prior to any unit in the sourcebook. Module 2 can conclude any unit that involves a significant public speaking component. Module 3 can be used to explore the specific theme of a youth-led service. Unit 5, Module 1, *Imaging Worship*, correlates somewhat to this unit; it explores an approach to understanding worship that is based on personal experience.

Unit outline

Content for Learning and Teaching
    Definitions of worship
        Specific elements
        Broad actions
        Sweeping movements
    The role of the worship leader
    Speaking words in worship
    The Christian year

Curriculum Modules
    Module 1: Worship: Where, Who, What, Why, and When?
    Module 2: The Role of the Worship Leader and Speaking Words in Worship
    Module 3: Thematic Worship and the Christian Year

Content for Learning and Teaching

What is worship?

The word *worship* comes from an earlier English term, *worth-ship*, which means to attribute worth or respect. The word *service*, meaning to do something for others, is closely connected to the idea of worship. Some churches use the word *liturgy* (literally "the work of the people") to talk about worship. These origins help to explain many definitions of worship, such as those found in two denominational resources:

Christian worship is the church's offering of love and praise to God.
    —*Minister's Manual* of the Mennonite Church (Canada and the United States)

Christian worship is an encounter with the triune God experienced in the midst of community, which transforms and empowers members of Christ's body for loving witness and service in the world.
    —Marlene Kropf, Rebecca Slough, and June Alliman Yoder, *Preparing Sunday Dinner*

Worship can also be explored by observing specific actions that occur when the Christian community is gathered, or by reflecting on the ultimate purpose of worship. This unit explores what worship is by focusing on the specific elements, broad actions, and sweeping movements of worship. The elements, actions, and movements included are examples, not an exhaustive list or specific requirements.

1. *Worship as specific elements*
   What happens when a faith community gathers?
   - Entering the worship space
   - Greeting one another
   - Call to worship
   - Opening prayer
   - Making/listening to music
   - Prayer of confession of sin
   - Words of assurance of forgiveness
   - Giving and receiving the offering
   - Time with children
   - Scripture reading
   - Dramatic or visual presentation
   - Sermon
   - Statement affirming faith
   - Witnessing/testifying
   - Rituals (such as baptism, communion, child dedication)
   - Sharing joys and concerns
   - Praying for the community and the world
   - Benediction/blessing
   - Announcements
   - Leaving the worship space

2) *Worship as broad actions:*
   What do the elements accomplish?
   - Gathering
   - Praising
   - Lamenting
   - Confessing
   - Reconciling
   - Praying
   - Offering ourselves and our gifts
   - Serving others
   - Receiving service
   - Hearing God's story
   - Responding to God's story
   - Sending

3) *Worship as sweeping movements*
   Worship can be defined in terms of three directions:
   - Vertical: encountering God
   - Horizontal: engaging the community and ourselves
   - Outward: empowering for faithful living in the world

The role of the worship leader

Preparing Sunday Dinner (see resource list, p. 12) describes worship leadership as corresponding to the three sweeping movements of worship: vertical, horizontal, and outward. The corresponding roles of worship leaders can be described as follows (with some adaptation of the material in *Preparing Sunday Dinner*):

1. Vertical: worship leader as *priest*
   Worship leaders are recognized by the community as filled with God's Spirit, familiar with its spiritual practices, and able to lead others to God.
2. Horizontal: worship leader as *host*
   Worship leaders care for the community and look after the organization of worship.
3. Outward: worship leader as *prophet*
   Worship leaders are truth tellers who care about the world God loves and help to inspire change in the world.

Speaking words in worship

Worship leaders will attend to the following principles of public speaking:

1. Voice
   - Speak slowly, clearly, and loudly.
   - Speak in a tone appropriate to the content of the text.
   - Rehearse out loud in advance.

2. Body
   - Stand still, balancing weight evenly on both feet and keeping your head straight.
   - Look up and make eye contact.
   - Communicate clearly with facial expressions.
   - Avoid distracting the congregation with grooming and clothing by keeping hair away from your face and not drawing attention to clothes.
   - Make purposeful gestures from the shoulder, not the elbow, eliminating random movements, especially if they are the result of nervousness.

3. Mind and soul
   - Listen to what you are saying and believe it.
   - Be authentic, urgent, expressive, and intentional.
   - Have passion and energy.
   - Your attitude is a model for congregation.

The Christian year

Advent is a season of longing and anticipation, during which we prepare for the coming of Jesus. The church year begins with Advent, starting four Sundays before Christmas.

Christmas is a day and a season when we celebrate God's coming among us as a human in Jesus, *Emmanuel* (which means "God with us"). Christmas lasts for 12 days, from December 25 to January 5.

Epiphany is celebrated on January 6, when we remember the magi's visit to the Christ child. During the time after Epiphany, we hear stories about Jesus' baptism and early ministry.

Lent is a season when we turn toward God and think about how our lives need to change. This is also a time to remember the gift of our baptism. Lent begins on Ash Wednesday and lasts for 40 days (not including Sundays), ending on the Saturday before Easter Sunday.

The Three Days are the most important part of the Christian calendar because they mark Jesus' last days, death and resurrection. These days (approximately three 24-hour periods) begin on Maundy Thursday evening and conclude on Easter evening.

On *Maundy Thursday* we hear the story of Jesus' last meal with his disciples and his act of service and love in washing their feet.

On *Good Friday* we hear of Jesus' trail, crucifixion, death, and burial.

On *Easter Sunday* we celebrate Jesus' resurrection and our new life in Christ. Easter falls on a different day each year, sometime between March 22 and April 25. *Easter* is not just one day, but a whole season to celebrate the resurrected Jesus. The season begins on Easter Sunday and lasts for 50 days (including Sundays).

The *Day of Pentecost* falls on the 50th day of the Easter season (Pentecost means 50th), when we honour the Holy Spirit and the church's mission in the world.

Time after Pentecost is the longest season in the church calendar, lasting almost half the year. Sometimes this is called "ordinary time."

Specific colours are associated with the seasons and days of the Christian year:
- Advent—violet or blue
- Christmas—white or gold
- Lent—violet
- Good Friday—black
- Easter season—white or gold
- Pentecost—red
- Ordinary time (time after Pentecost, time after Epiphany)—green

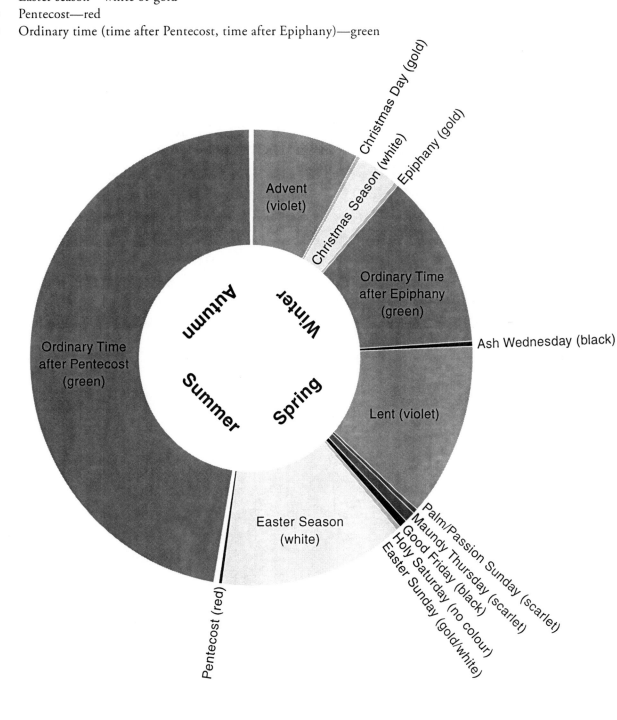

Resources

Worship and worship leadership

Kreider, Eleanor. *Enter His Gates: Fitting Worship Together*. Scottdale, PA: Herald Press, 1990.

Ramshaw, Gail. *Christian Worship: 100,000 Sundays of Symbols and Rituals*. Minneapolis: Fortress Press, 2009.

Rempel, John, ed. *Minister's Manual*. Scottdale, PA: Herald Press, 1998.

White, James F. *Introduction to Christian Worship*. Nashville: Abingdon Press, 2000.

Yoder, June Alliman, Marlene Kropf, and Rebecca Slough. *Preparing Sunday Dinner: A Collaborative Approach to Worship and Preaching*. Scottdale, PA: Herald Press, 2005.

The Christian year

Duerksen, Carol. *Sacred Search: Encountering God during Advent*. Scottdale, PA: Faith & Life Resources, 2005.

Iona Community and Wild Goose Worship Group. *Cloth for the Cradle: Worship Resources and Readings for Advent, Christmas & Epiphany*. Chicago: GIA Publications, 2000.

Iona Community and Wild Goose Worship Group. *Stages on the Way: Worship Resources for Lent, Holy Week & Easter*. Chicago: GIA Publications, 2000.

Johns, Helen. *Celebrating Advent*. Bible Studies for Junior High. Newton, KS: Faith & Life Press, 1994.

Kehrberg, Sarah, ed. *The Mennonite Handbook*. Scottdale, PA: Herald Press, 2007.

Revised Common Lectionary: The Consultation on Common Texts. Nashville: Abingdon, 1998. Web link: http://divinity.library.vanderbilt.edu/lectionary/

Reed, Angela. *Sacred Search: Encountering God during Lent*. Scottdale, PA: Faith & Life Resources, 2004.

Stookey, Laurence Hull. *Calendar: Christ's Time for the Church*. Nashville: Abingdon Press, 1996.

Worship:
Where, Who, What, Why, and When?

Module focus

What is worship? Where and when do we worship? Who does what in worship? Why worship? This module links the elements of Sunday worship with the ultimate purpose of worship—encountering God, one another, and the world.

Leader preparation

Materials

- Set of markers
- 7 to 10 envelopes *or* folders for each small group
- For *Opening Option 2*: newsprint, letter-sized paper, drawing tools
- Writing and drawing instruments
- Visual focus and distinctive sound maker (see *Introduction*, p. 6)
- For *Reflection Time*:
    - —Index card, one per youth.
    - —Strips of cardboard or wooden tongue depressors (big enough to write on), enough for two per youth
    - —Something to connect the two pieces (wire, tape, etc.), index card
    - —Play dough or modelling clay, enough for a small fist-sized lump for each youth
    - —Music player and music (for example: *Sanctuary*—John W. Thompson, Randy Scruggs, 1982, *Everyday*—Phillips Craig Dean, Hillsong 1999, *Here I Am to Worship*—Tim Hughes)

Tasks

- Familiarize yourself with the *Content for Learning and Teaching** on defining worship.
- If necessary, reserve the church's sanctuary for the opening activity.
- For *Opening activity option 2** create a diagram of your church's worship space. It will resemble the game Battleship, and should include:
    - —10 x 10 grid in the area where the congregation is seated, labelled with numbers down one side and letters across on the top
    - —Aisles, pulpits, musical instruments, sound booths, etc.
    - —List of church members who must be found beside the diagram (one family of five, one family of four, one family of three, one group of three friends, and one couple)
    - —Make two large diagrams on newsprint and two small copies on letter paper. See below for game instructions.
- *Reflection and prayer*
    - —Set up the visual focus and distinctive sound maker.*

---

*   See page 6 in the introduction for the suggested use of a distinctive sound and visual focus or worship centre for your *Reflection and prayer* time.

Session

Opening activity: Who? Where? (15 minutes)

Option 1: The sanctuary game

This activity gives the youth an opportunity to explore and become comfortable in the church sanctuary. A minimum of six players is required.

How to play:

- Select one seeker. The seeker stands on a chair or pew in the centre of the sanctuary.
- Once the seeker's feet are planted, they cannot move, but he or she can twist and bend.
- The seeker shuts his or her eyes and counts down from ten, while the other players hide in the worship space where they cannot be seen by the seeker.
- The seeker then tries to locate the hiders and identify them aloud by name and location.
- Once no more hiders can be spotted, the seeker closes eyes, holds arms out to the sides and counts down again, beginning with eight.
- This time the hiders must run, touch the seeker's arms and hide again before the seeker reaches one. When the seeker stops counting, everyone must stay where they are.
- Each countdown begins with a progressively lower number, until hiders are forced to hide close to the seeker in order to touch his or her hand during the countdown. The last hider to be found wins and is the seeker in the next round.

Bring the group back together and ask each youth to name one spot in the sanctuary (no repetitions). Who would be there during the worship service, and what would that person be doing on Sunday morning?

Option 2: Blackout in the Sanctuary

This game is based on the classic pen and paper game Battleship. It asks participants to imagine a blackout during a worship service, requiring that candles be distributed to church members scattered throughout the sanctuary.

How to play:

- Divide the group into two teams.
- Give each a letter-sized diagram and a copy of the larger version.
- Using their letter-sized diagram, each team secretly "hides" their church members in the worship space, marking their locations on the grid.
- The teams take turns guessing where the opposing team's church members are located.
- On the larger diagrams, they draw an X in each empty square and stick figure in each square where a church member is found.
- If a church member is located, the successful team continues guessing until they encounter an empty square.
- The first team to locate all of the hidden groups wins.

Following the game, use the diagram to discuss who would be where and what they would be doing during the service.

Discussion: What? When? Why? (20 minutes)

Part 1: Specific elements of worship (5 minutes)

- Divide the youth into groups of three to five.
- Give each group some markers and about 20 index cards or strips of paper.
- Instruct each group to think of as many things that happen during the worship service as they can and write one on each card. Encourage them to be as comprehensive as possible, including small details and items not listed in an order of service.
- When the groups have finished listing these parts of worship, ask them to arrange the cards in the order in which the elements normally occur in the service.
- Gather as a large group to compare collections of elements.

Option

For a younger or less focused group, you provide the elements and ask the groups to arrange them in the order they occur during the service.

Part 2: Broad actions accomplished by each element (5 minutes)

Return to the same small groups and ask the youth to sort the elements into categories, based on what functions they accomplish. For example, the sermon, time with children, and Scripture reading could all be associated with the action of telling God's story, teaching, or learning. Similarly, the opening prayer, confession, and congregational prayer could be grouped under praying. or talking and listening to God. Provide additional strips of paper or index cards, so elements can be copied and included in more than one action category. Use envelopes or folders to group the categories, labelling them appropriately. Provide hints if necessary.

When the groups have finished sorting elements, gather again to compare and discuss the results. Use these questions to guide the discussion.

1. What categories were used by more than one group?
2. What elements fit into more than one category?
3. Are there elements that do not fit into any of the categories the groups identified?
4. Are action categories missing that you would expect to find in a worship service?
5. If your congregation uses a printed order of worship, is the service divided into different action categories? If your congregation uses a hymnal structured according to the broad actions of worship (such as *Hymnal: A Worship Book*) how does the structure of the table of contents in the hymnal correspond to the categories developed by the groups?

Option

To simplify this activity, you may provide categories for the youth to fill in with elements, rather than asking them to develop their own. If so, list them on the board or on newsprint.

Part 3: Sweeping movements behind these actions (10 minutes)

Teaching moment: One way to define worship is to list the specific things we do in worship and name the actions they represent. It is also important to think about the purpose behind these actions.

There are three main reasons we worship:

1. To encounter God: vertical/up and down
2. To connect with the community and examine ourselves: horizontal/side to side
3. To be empowered for faithful living in the world: outward

Small group discussion

Return to small discussion groups and ask each group to write down on the envelopes or folders how each of their broad action categories is vertical, horizontal, and outward.

For example, teaching or telling God's story:
- Vertical: enables us to learn more about who God is and deepen our relationships with God
- Horizontal: learn from each other as a community and reflect on who we are as individuals in relation to God
- Outward: learn how to live as Christians in the world

Large group discussion

Gather and invite each group to report. The results should connect the specific elements and broad actions of Christian worship to the formation of relationships between God, the community, and the world.

Option

Instead of connecting every action to the movements, the primary elements of the service can be divided among the groups and each element related to the vertical, horizontal, and outward aspects of worship. For example, in congregational prayer we encounter God, since as the prayer is addressed to God; we engage with one another in praying for each other's joys and concerns; and we are empowered to serve the world through praying for situations of global need and celebration.

Reflection: Worship in daily life (10 minutes)

Teaching moment: One symbol of the way the vertical, horizontal, and outward dimensions come together when we worship (and not just on Sundays) is the cross. It is vertical, horizontal, and rooted in the world.

- *Reflection*: Give each youth two beams to make a cross, wire or tape to attach them, a marker, an index card or small piece of paper, and a piece of play dough or clay that allows the cross to stand upright on the card.
- Instruct them to use the markers to write on the beams the ways they plan to worship God this week.
   —Vertical beam: pray at bedtime, pray before meals
   —Horizontal beam: memorize Scripture passage, journal about my spiritual life, ask Grandmother about her faith journey.
- Use the index card or paper to list ways they will worship God through their daily outward actions (reuse grocery bags, recycle, give a contribution to a charity).
- Make the distinctive sound and ask them to begin.
- After five minutes, make the distinctive sound.
- Ask the group to place their crosses around the visual centre.
- Close in prayer. Example:
   God, we thank you for the opportunity we have to worship you when we gather with our congregation on Sunday morning. We also thank you that we can worship you all week, through setting aside time to spend with you and caring for other people and the world, through the power of your Spirit, Amen.
- Youth may take their crosses as a reminder of worship in daily life.

Option

Instead of making upright crosses, distribute papers with the simple outline of a cross with a circle around the centre indicating vertical, horizontal, and outward dimensions.

The Role of the Worship Leader and Speaking Words in Worship

Module focus

What is the role of the worship leader? Module 2 explores the leader's role as a priest, host, and prophet. This module can be used to prepare the youth for any spoken contribution to worship resulting from another module.

Leader preparation

Materials

- Basket, list of occupations (p. 20)
- Chalkboard and chalk *or* chart paper and markers
- Stopwatch or timer
- Chart paper/markers
- Paper, pens
- Copies of spoken worship resource, one for each participant. This may be a piece prepared by the group in another unit, or one selected from another source. It should lend itself to multiple readers, or to unison or antiphonal reading. Examples are a prayer from the back of *Hymnal: A Worship Book*, a litany from a recent bulletin, or a reader's theatre. Ideally, the resource will be one that the youth could contribute to the next Sunday worship service.

Tasks

- *Opening activity*
  —Copy the list of occupations on page 20 and cut it into strips, each with one occupation. Place the strips in the basket and set it near the chalkboard or flip chart at the front of the room.
- *Discussion*
  —Write the three descriptions of worship leaders and the three questions (p. 18) for Part 2 of the discussion on chart paper. Provide paper and pens for each small group.
- *Preparing for worship*
  —Collaborate with worship planners to select a worship resource (prayer, reading, or reader's theatre) for the youth to contribute to worship. Reserve the worship space, so you can practice.

Session

Opening activity: Speed Pictionary (10 minutes)

Speed Pictionary explores how different occupations relate to the role of worship leader:

- Divide the group into teams of equal numbers.
- One team sends a drawer to the chalkboard.
- The drawer picks a slip out of the basket and tries to get the team to guess as many occupations as possible using only drawings (no numbers or letters, actions, or spoken words).
- When the team guesses correctly, the drawer picks another slip. This continues for 20 seconds.
- When the timer sounds, the other team takes a turn.
- Continue playing until every person has a chance to draw.
- The team with the most points wins.
- Scoring:
    - —Win one point for each successful guess
    - —Lose one point for each rule violation
    - —Lose two points if you skip an occupation

Option for smaller groups

One person draws and the entire group guesses. One point is awarded to the guesser and one the drawer for each successful guess.

Variation

Speed Charades, in which the occupations are acted out rather than drawn.

Discussion: The role of the worship leader (18 minutes)

Part 1: Discussing the game (5 minutes)

At the end of the game each youth finds a partner. Each pair is assigned one of the occupations and given one minute to answer the following question:

How is being a _____ like being a worship leader?

Then have each pair share their response with the group. Hopefully the youth will come up with creative ideas and images. For example: being a worship leader is like being a professional football player because it involves training and practice over a long period of time, or it is like being a plumber because if anything goes wrong, it is your job to repair the damage.

Part 2: The three dimensions of worship leadership (13 minutes)
Teaching moment: Worship leaders have to think in three dimensions:

1. *Vertically, about the relationship between the community, individuals and God*
2. *Horizontally, about the relationships between people in the community*
3. *Outwardly, about the relationship between the community, individuals and the world*

Depending on the size of your group, divide into three or six groups. Give each group one of these three written descriptions of a worship leader:

- Worship leaders are recognized by the community as filled with God's Spirit, familiar with its spiritual practices, and able to lead others to God.
- Worship leaders care for the community and look after the organization of worship.
- Worship leaders are truth tellers who care about the world God loves and help inspire change in the world.

Refer to the board or flip chart with these three questions for groups to address in relation to their descriptions:
- How do worship leaders do this during the worship service?
- How do worship leaders prepare to do this before the worship service?
- What occupation would be a good image for this role of the worship leader? (Ex. carpenter, pilot, etc.)

Following the small group time, gather as a large group. Read each description, and ask the appropriate group to share their response briefly. After each topic, inform the group of the images used in the *Content for Learning and Teaching*: priest, host and prophet.

Preparing for worship: Speaking words in worship (15 minutes)

Distribute copies of a spoken worship resource (see supplies, p. 17). Then prepare the youth to lead this part of worship.
1. Review the basics of speaking words in worship in *Content for Learning and Teaching*.
2. Rehearse it, ideally in the worship space itself. Determine where each person will stand and how individuals will move in and out of position.
3. If a sound system will be used, ensure each person has access to a microphone and can be clearly heard. If possible, practice with the sound system.
4. If there is a group refrain or congregational response, arrange how you will begin and end together. Think about the length of pauses between each section and line.
5. Make sure everyone understands content and logistics. It is necessary for leaders to comprehend what is said and avoid distracting behaviour for the congregation to understand and focus.

Option 1

If members of your group are uncomfortable speaking alone, consider inviting them to lead a congregational refrain with a hand gesture or help operate the sound system.

Option 2

If your group isn't comfortable leading a service or is not planning to lead a service, have them practice reading worship resources just to gain experience in public speaking.

Prayer of preparation (2 minutes)

As you conclude this practice session, offer a short, spoken prayer thanking God for the opportunity to lead worship and asking for guidance as worship is prepared and practiced. Example:

Generous God, thank you for giving us the opportunity to lead our congregation in worship. Help us to be priests, hosts, and prophets (add your group's imagery), so our community can encounter you, one another, and the world. Amen.

Occupations

Accountant	Construction worker	Nurse
Actor	Dancer	Optician
Air traffic controller	Dentist	Pharmacist
Archaeologist	Disc jockey	Photographer
Artist	Doctor (MD)	Physicist
Astronomer	Editor	Pilot
Author	Electrician	Police officer
Babysitter	Engineer	Politician
Baggage porter	Farmer	Professional athlete
Baker	Fashion designer	Psychologist
Bank teller	Firefighter	Real estate agent
Biologist	Fisherman	Reporter
Bodyguard	Flight attendant	Roofer
Butcher	Florist	Secretary
Cab driver	Grocer	Singer
Cardiologist	Hairdresser	Social worker
Carpenter	Interior designer	Teacher
Chef	Jeweller	Truck Driver
Cleaning staff	Judge	Veterinarian
Coach	Lawyer	Waiter/Waitress
Comedian	Librarian	Webmaster
Computer programmer	Lifeguard	X-ray technician

Thematic Worship
and the Christian Year

Module focus

How are themes and topics for worship chosen? How can worship explore a theme or topic? This module illustrates the use of the Christian year to determine worship themes and introduces youth to basic worship planning resources. It can also be used to explore alternative themes.

Leader preparation

Materials

- White candle
- Crepe paper streamers, ribbon, yarn, etc., in colours of Christian year
- Narrow sheets of paper (2.5 inches/6 cm wide)
- Pens or pencils for everyone
- Labels for seasons of Christian year (see Christian year diagram, p. 11)
- Paper
- Copy of the handout (p. 24) for each participant
- Bibles, hymnals, books of Christian art (libraries usually have a wide selection)
- Visual focus and sound maker*
- Music player, seasonal music (optional)

Tasks

- *Visual focus*
    - —Using the diagram on page 11 as a guide, create a room-sized visual on the floor to help the group to visualize the Christian year.
    - —Place the white candle in the centre of the floor.
    - —Arrange the streamers, ribbon, or yarn in the colours of the seasons of the Christian year around the candle. Try to represent the proportion of the year identified with each season.
    - —Create as large a visual as possible, given the space available and the size of your group.
- *Opening activity*
    - —Write phrases at the top along the short edge of the narrow sheets of paper. (Suggested phrases: "Jesus washing the disciples' feet," "Fast food combo meal," "We all live in a yellow submarine," "Christmas Eve candlelight service," "National Hockey League playoffs," "16th birthday cake.")
- *Discussion*
    - —If you choose the option of a matching game, prepare a list of Scriptures or hymns from which to choose for each season (see p. 22).
- *Reflection and prayer*
    - —Prepare a brief time of reflection and prayer based on the current season of the Christian year.

---

* See page 6 in the introduction for the suggested use of a distinctive sound and visual focus or worship centre for your *Reflection and prayer* time.

Session

Opening activity: Picto-telephone (10 minutes)

Play Picto-telephone to introduce phrases related to the Christian year. Sit in a circle around the visual focus. Distribute one narrow sheet of paper, with a phrase written at the top, to each person. Explain how to complete the exercise, demonstrating the following steps:

1. The first person folds the paper so the phrase is hidden and draws a picture representing the phrase on the back.
2. He/she passes the paper to the next person.
3. This person folds the paper so the picture is covered and writes a phrase describing the picture on the back.

Allow 10 or 15 seconds to complete each task. After each sheet of paper is full, or the entire circle has contributed, open the papers. Compare the initial phrases and the ending phrases.

Discussion: Exploring seasons of the Christian year (30 minutes)

Teaching moment: Christmas and Easter are important times in the Christian year. Our church celebrates Christmas and Easter, and therefore we celebrate the Christian year. Shaping worship based on certain seasons and days is one way to walk through the life of Jesus each year in worship as a community of faith. Add labels to each colour in the central visual while offering a one sentence explanation of each season and day (see Content for Learning and Teaching, *p. 8).*

Small group discussion (10 minutes)
- Distribute Bibles, hymnals, handout (p. 24), and books of art.
- Invite individuals or pairs sitting in (or opposite) each portion of the circle to choose a Scripture text, hymn or song, and piece of art that is relevant to that season in the Christian year.
    —Have people in "Ordinary Time" pick a theme for their focus.
    —If necessary, ask each individual or pair to look at several related seasons and days (for example, Advent and Christmas, or Good Friday and Easter).

Option 1

With a group less familiar with Scripture and church music, play a matching game by providing a list of appropriate Scripture excerpts, hymns, and art works. Have the youth look through and select ones that match their days or seasons.

Option 2

With a smaller group, have everyone walk around the circle in a group and together choose Scripture, music, and art for each season.

Large group sharing (15 minutes)

Ask each pair to share their Scripture text, hymn or song, and piece of art, and explain their choices. Consider reading excerpts from Scripture, songs, or hymns. Sing the songs, if your group is musical.

Personal reflection (5 minutes)

It is also important to explore themes not included in the Christian year. During a time of quiet reflection accompanied by music, give each youth a 3 x 5 card and ask them to write down themes they wish were addressed in worship. Pass the suggestions on to the worship committee or a pastor.

Option

Instead of writing the themes down, simply allow the youth to share them verbally while one person writes them down.

Reflection and prayer: Celebrating the current season (5 minutes)

Gather around the visual focus. Lead the group in a time of prayer and reflection based on the current season of the Christian year. Draw on resources such as those listed in *Content for Learning and Teaching* (p. 8). Consider playing seasonal music, including a brief Scripture reading, spoken prayer, or ritual action. Use your distinctive sound to begin and end the time of prayer.

✂ -

Celebrating the Christian Year

Season or Day in the Christian Year:

Description of season or day:

Scripture:

Song:

Art:

Other:

✂ -

Celebrating the Christian Year

Season or Day in the Christian Year:

Description of season or day:

Scripture:

Song:

Art:

Other:

✂ -

Celebrating the Christian Year

Season or Day in the Christian Year:

Description of season or day:

Scripture:

Song:

Art:

Other:

✂ -

Opening and Closing Worship

Unit focus

In many worshipping communities, the beginning and ending of a service are carefully planned, whether it starts when the first person sits down beside a campfire in silence or ends with an elaborate recessional. A service often begins and ends with words or music. This unit explores choosing and writing words for worship, and different ways to open or close a worship service. By the end of this unit, you will have worship openings and closings that are written by your class.

Language is an integral part of worship. A thorough exploration of worship language is included in this unit, which can serve as a reference when working through the other modules. As noted in the introduction, it is possible to combine the curriculum modules in different ways, based on the time available and the interests and abilities of the youth. To focus on opening and closing the service, use Module 1 and Module 3. Modules 2 and 3 help the class design worship actions that can be used in your congregation.

Unit outline

Content for Learning and Teaching
    Opening worship
    Closing worship
    Choosing words for worship
    Language for worship
    More than words
    Resources

Curriculum Modules
    Module 1: Opening and Closing Worship
    Module 2: Worship Language and Finding Words for Worship
    Module 3: Writing Opening and Closing Words Together

Youth Worship Leadership Suggestions
    Getting creative
    Youth worship leadership checklist: Opening and closing the service

Content for Learning and Teaching

Opening worship

There are two important aspects of every opening:
1. Recognizing one another as members of the gathered community of faith
2. Inviting the congregation into the presence of God

These can be addressed through the same element or through two separate elements. If you use more than one, each element should have a clear and unique purpose. The opening can also introduce the theme of the service and establish a context for the central actions of the service. It is important to keep the opening simple and brief.

Examples of opening elements:
- Formal greeting ("God be with you" and the response "And also with you")
- Informal words of welcome ("Good morning! Welcome here this summer Sunday.")
- Call to worship (*Hymnal: A Worship Book* 662)
- Opening prayer or invocation (*HWB* 674)
- Collect (short, traditional structured prayer, *HWB* 732)
- Confession and assurance (*HWB* 698, *HWB* 706)
- Silence, with or without a focus statement
- Movement or ritual (lighting candles, kneeling)
- Greeting one another and shaking hands
- Prelude
- Procession (worship leaders enter with objects such a cross or Bible)
- Gathering music ("Here in this place," Marty Haugen, 1981 *HWB* 6; "Come, now is the time to worship," Brian Doerksen, 1998)
- Visual display
- Announcements

Closing worship

The closing has two important aspects as well:
1. Commissioning: challenging the congregation to follow through with the call to action expressed in the service ("Go and . . .")
2. Blessing: extending the gift of God's peace, love and empowerment to all ("May God . . .")

As with the opening, these can be addressed through the same element or through two separate elements. If using more than one, each element should have a clear and unique purpose. You can restate the theme of the service at this time.

Examples of closing elements:
- Benediction (blessing, *HWB* 772)
- Commission (*HWB* 763)
- Closing prayer (*HWB* 765)
- Silence
- Movement or ritual
- Recessional (people leading worship leave with objects such a cross or Bible)
- Sending music (blessing—"God be with you till we meet again," Jeremiah Rankin, 1880 *HWB* 430; commissioning—"Heart with loving heart united," Nicolaus L. Von Zinzendorf, trans. Walter Klassen, 1983 *HWB* 420)
- Postlude

Worship resources

Worship resources are texts intended to be used for different parts of worship, such as prayers, responsive readings, and rituals or actions. These resources can be presented by a worship leader, or several readers, or the entire congregation. Many hymnals, including *Hymnal: A Worship Book*, include worship resources.

Choosing words for worship

Scan collections of worship resources for texts that fit the theme of the service and their use in the service. When you discover a text that may be appropriate, read it aloud to yourself and consider the following questions:
- Can you understand the text the first time you read it? Do you know immediately and precisely what all the words mean?
- Does the text have a good rhythm? Is it awkward to read the text out loud?

Read the text again and consider the following questions:

- How does the text relate to the theme of the service? What words and phrases connect to the scripture reading and theme? How does it add? How does it distract? (consider central Scripture readings, images, and ideas)
- How does the text fulfill its role in the service? Does it address God or the congregation? Which element does it fit (recognizing each other, recognizing God, blessing and commissioning)?
- Imagine the congregation hearing or speaking the text. Is it an honest expression of the faith of the community? Would anyone feel alienated or hurt by the words? Does it use inclusive language for humanity and God? Review *Language for Worship* in Unit 4 (p. 65).
- What would you change about the resource? Could the text be used in combination with another worship resource?

If the opening or closing is spoken by a leader or printed in the bulletin, feel free to edit the text by changing words or removing or adding sections. You may wish to combine two or more texts. For evaluating and altering texts, see the comments on writing words for worship, Unit 4, page 64.

Resources

The beginning and end of the service

The Worship Sourcebook. Grand Rapids, Michigan: Baker Books, 2004.

Yoder, June Alliman, Marlene Kropf and Rebecca Slough. *Preparing Sunday Dinner: A Collaborative Approach to Worship and Preaching*. Scottdale, PA: Herald Press, 2005.

Worship resources

Case, Steven L. *The Book of Uncommon Prayer*. El Cajon, CA: Youth Specialties, 2002.

Hymnal: A Worship Book. Scottdale, PA: Mennonite Publishing House, 1992.

Leader magazine. Scottdale, PA: Faith and Life Resources.

Mark, Arlene M. *Words for Worship*. Scottdale, PA: Herald Press, 1996.

Iona Community resources:. Available from Wild Goose Publications and GIA Publications.

Sing the Journey. Hymnal: A Worship Book—Supplement I. Scottdale, PA: Faith & Life Resources, 2005.

Sing the Story. Hymnal: A Worship Book—Supplement II. Scottdale, PA: Faith & Life Resources, 2007.

The Worship Sourcebook. Grand Rapids: Baker Books, 2004.

Zaerr Brenneman, Diane. *Words for Worship 2*. Scottdale PA: Herald Press, 2009.

Writing worship resources

Duck, Ruth C. *Finding Words for Worship: A Guide for Leaders*. Louisville: Westminster John Knox Press, 1995.

Stookey, Laurence Hull. *Let the Whole Church Say Amen: A Guide for Those Who Pray in Public*. Nashville: Abingdon Press, 2001.

Opening and Closing Worship

Module focus

How do we start and end worship services? Module 1 invites youth to:

1. Evaluate current practices
2. Consider creative alternatives
3. Practice blessing and commissioning each other

Leader preparation

Materials

*   Printed orders of worship from previous services
*   Bibles, hymnals, song lyrics, etc., used in the services
*   Copy of handout (p. 31) for each participant
*   Chalkboard and chalk *or* chart paper and markers
*   Music player and reflective music
*   Musical version of Numbers 6:24-26 (see tasks, below)
*   Visual focus (candle, plant, flower, bowl, etc) and sound maker*
*   Slips of paper
*   Pens/pencils
*   Stopwatch

Tasks

*   *Discussion*
    —If a printed order of worship is not used in your congregation, ask for several outlines of the beginning of worship services from a regular worship leader. If possible, provide a copy of the words used by the worship leader.
    —Review *Content for Learning and Teaching* (p. 25) and select ways of beginning and ending worship that are unfamiliar in your congregation.. These elements will be used by small groups in the second part of the discussion.
*   *Reflection and prayer*
    —Select music for the time of reflection. (Suggestions: "Christ's is the world," John Bell, 1989, *Sing the Journey* CD 2; "The kingdom of God is justice and peace," Taizé Community; "One is the body," John Bell, *Sing the Journey* CD 1)
    —Find a musical version of Numbers 6:24-26, "May the Lord bless you and keep you." ("For the journey," by Steve Bell; "The Lord bless you and keep you," composed by John Rutter)
    —Write the two closing worship actions on chart paper or a chalkboard.
    —Prepare a visual focus and select a distinctive sound (bell, rainstick, gong, guitar chord, etc.). Pick a place for the visual focus element.
*   Consider inviting a worship leader to join the group for this module.

---

* See page 6 in the introduction for the suggested use of a distinctive sound and visual focus or worship centre for your *Reflection and prayer* time.

Session

Opening activity: Theme Game (12 minutes)

The Theme Game is a way to explore a topic from a range of perspectives. It is an improvisational drama game in which teams of youth act out short vignettes on a theme (under 30 seconds each). For example, vignettes on the theme "light" could include: Edison discovering the light bulb, watching a sunrise, eating nonfat yogurt, or singing "This little light of mine" with actions.

- Divide the youth into two even teams.
- Announce the theme and give both teams 30 seconds to brainstorm ideas.
- The teams then take turns presenting vignettes (under 30 seconds each).
- A leader counts to five in between vignettes to allow time to get organized.
- The first group that fails to come up with a new idea loses.

It's easy to add youth to the teams while the game is in progress. Use the theme "peace" or "light" to warm up and then try "beginning," the theme that introduces the module. Other themes to explore include: power, energy, growth, foundations, instructions, journeys, structure, strength, seasons, community, communication, connections and tension.

Option

With fewer than six youth, consider playing the game as one large group. If your group doesn't like to act, consider brainstorming on the theme "beginning." Give each person a piece of paper. Tell them to write down the first three words that come to mind when you say a word. When everyone is ready, say the word "beginning." Allow five seconds to write. Ask youth to say the words out loud and explain how they relate to "beginning."

Discussion (20 minutes)

Part 1: Current practice (10 minutes)

Divide the youth into small groups of two to four and give each group a bulletin or worship outline from a different service. Give the groups the resources required to interpret the order of worship (hymnal, song lyrics, copy of the call to worship, etc.) and *Handout 1* (p. 31). Have the groups answer each of the questions.

Call the groups back together and briefly share their results.

Teaching moment: Two actions begin worship:
1. *recognizing each other as a worshipping community*
2. *recognizing God's presence*

Write the actions on the board or chart paper. Ask: How does this congregation accomplish the two primary actions of the opening of the service?

Part 2: Exploring different options (10 minutes)

Now that you have evaluated your congregation's worship practices, look at other options. From the list provided in *Content for Learning and Teaching* (pp. 25-27), choose elements not often used in your congregation. Assign one small group of two to four youth to discuss each of these elements. Provide a clear description and example of the element. Ask groups to discuss the following:

How does beginning the service in this way . . .
1. Recognize each other as a worshipping community?
2. Recognize God's presence?

Give the groups time to discuss the questions, and then gather to share ideas. Understanding the value of different ways of opening a worship service can enrich worship in the congregation and also experiences in encountering other Christian traditions.

Option

If time allows, or if the sending is the group's primary involvement in the worship service, do a similar exercise for the end of the service.

Reflection and prayer (13 minutes)

Give youth the opportunity to commission one another and receive a blessing.

Teaching moment: Two actions happen at the end of a worship service:
1. *Commissioning: We challenge the community to live as Christians in the world and take action based on the message of the service.*
2. *Blessing: We extend the gift of God's peace, love, and empowerment to others*
Write the actions on the board where they are visible to all.

Write these statements on the board:
- What are you doing in the next week?
- Is God asking you to do anything special or different this week?
- Think of a sentence or phrase that summarizes God's call or commission to you: "God calls us to . . ."

Distribute pencils and ask the group to write answers to these questions on their papers. When they hear the distinctive sound, they should gather around the visual focus.

You can use this example to illustrate the activity:

There's a guy, John, in one of my classes who disagrees with me. When we're having a discussion, I'm usually thinking about how I can argue with him, instead of really listening to what he has to say. So the commission I share is: "God calls us to listen to others without being distracted by planning what to say in response."

Begin the music for reflection. After five minutes, make the sound and invite everyone back to the visual focus.

Commission one another

Say, "God calls us to follow Jesus in our everyday lives not only when we are together." Read your own statement, and then ask each person to read their own statements written during the reflection time. (Suggestion: Go around the circle rather than waiting for people to volunteer.) Say, "God calls us to follow."

Bless the group with the following words:
May God who made all things
and makes all things new
guide us and give us life.

As youth leave, play a musical setting of Numbers 6:24-26.

How We Open Worship?

1. What do the first words in the service tell us about worship?
   Are the words from Scripture?
   Are they spoken to God or about God?
   Are they spoken to the congregation?
   Are they casual or formal?
   Do they relate to the time of the church year?
   Are announcements presented?
   What does all of this mean?

2. What does the music used at the beginning of the service tell us about worship?
   Is it related to the theme of the service?
   Is it sung to God or about God?
   Is it about the congregation?
   Is it energetic or reflective?
   If you were a visitor would it be easy or hard to sing?
   Is it familiar or new to the congregation?
   What does all of this mean?

3. What else happened at the beginning of the service, and what does this tell us about worship?
   Is there movement?
   Is there ritual?
   Is there a visual display?
   Is there a time of reflection or silence?
   Do people greet one another?
   Does the congregation sit or stand?
   What does all of this mean?

4. What secular event does the beginning of worship most resemble and why? (Rock concert, court room, family dinner, etc.)

Worship Language
and Finding Words for Worship

Module focus

How do we find and evaluate words to use in worship? Module 2 presents a method for finding and evaluating worship resources in general, or for a particular theme and Scripture text.

Leader preparation

Materials

- Copies of *Handout 1* (p. 35), enough for half the class
- Pens/pencils
- Copies of *Handout 2* (p. 36), one for each participant
- Hymnals, Bibles, worship resources
- Play dough (buy or make with basic kitchen ingredients; find recipes online)
- Visual focus
- Distinctive sound maker
- Music player, quiet instrumental music

Tasks

- *Opening Activity*
    —Make copies of handouts.
- Familiarize yourself with *Content for Learning and Teaching on Worship Resources* (p. 25) and *Choosing Words For Worship* (p. 26).
- *Discussion*
    —Choose and post a Scripture text and theme, based on one or more of the following:
    - Scripture text and theme for the following Sunday service
    - Service the youth will be leading after completing the unit
    - Current Bible study topics
    - If none of the above: Matthew 7:7-8 on the theme of "seeking God"; Genesis 1:1-5, "God creates light"; or Matthew 22:36-40, "Love God and neighbour."
- Consider inviting a worship leader to join the group for this module.
- Post the two important aspects of opening worship and two important aspects for closing worship from the *Content for Learning and Teaching* (pp. 25-26).

---

*   See page 6 in the introduction for the suggested use of a distinctive sound and visual focus or worship centre for your *Reflection and prayer* time.

Session

Opening activity: Crossword puzzle race (15 minutes)

Option 1

Wait until everyone arrives, then divide the youth into pairs and give each pair a copy of the puzzle (*Handout 1*). The first pair to complete the puzzle wins. If 10 minutes have passed and no one has finished, the pair with the most correct words wins.

Option 2

Divide the group into pairs as they arrive. Give each pair a copy of the puzzle and ask them to solve it. Add pairs as more people arrive. Work in pairs for five minutes. If no one has solved the puzzle, work on it as a group.

Option 3

Work on the puzzle as a group.

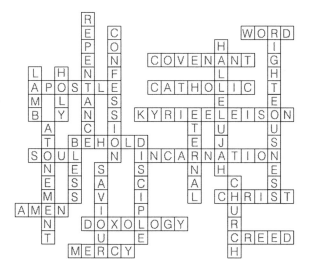

Teaching Moment: The words found in the crossword puzzle are used often in worship, yet rarely in daily life. It is important to understand what we are saying during worship. It is also important to avoid using words in worship just because they sound religious.

Discussion: Choosing words for worship (23 minutes)

This section provides an opportunity for youth to find opening and closing words on a specific theme and Scripture text. They will also evaluate the effectiveness of their chosen words.

Small group discussion (15 minutes)

Teaching moment: Worship leaders often find words to use in worship, rather than writing their own. The words are often borrowed from collections of worship resources, prayers, and readings that are suitable for many different worship services and worshipping communities.

Introduce the Scripture and theme and explain the process for choosing words for worship described on *Handout 2*. Emphasize that groups do not need to find the perfect worship resource, only one they can evaluate. They don't need to like the worship resource. It may be more interesting to evaluate a resource they dislike.

Divide into small groups of two to four. Ask half of the groups to find opening words and the other half closing words. Give each group the handout and resources, including the denominational hymnal and songbooks (if they include worship elements) and at least one other collection of worship resources.

Option

If words are not spoken to open and close worship in your congregation, consider searching for resources on a theme/Scripture that could be incorporated into another element of the service or the sermon.

Large group sharing (8 minutes)

Gather as a large group and share the results of the small group discussions.

Poll the group on the following questions and discuss the results. Make it clear that there are no right answers and that worship is continually evolving and changing:

1. Was it hard to find good worship resources? No or Yes
   Why? What was good about what was there? What was missing?
2. Did you find it easy to relate to these worship resources? No or Yes
   Why? What made it easy? What made it difficult?

Reflection and prayer (7 minutes)

Teaching moment: Words are important in worship, but they are not everything. All of our senses should be engaged in worship—through art, movement, touch, music, relationship, and more. We encounter God with our bodies, emotions, and intellects. Yet God is beyond our reality or our comprehension, and most definitely beyond our words. This time of reflection and prayer is a chance to explore other ways of connecting with God through touch, sight, and hearing.

Gather around the visual focus. Give each person a piece of play dough and ask them to make an image representing what God means to them at this time in their life. Youth can sit anywhere in the room while they work.

Begin a time of quiet reflection with the distinctive sound and play quiet instrumental music as they work. After three to five minutes, stop the music and invite the group to gather and place their sculptures around the visual centre, then stand quietly. After a minute of silence, mark the end of silent prayer with the sound.

Worship Words

ACROSS

3   (a) Jesus, (b) Bible, (c) preaching
6   A treaty, pact or contract
9   One who is sent, a messenger (for example, Paul of Tarsus)
10 Universal, worldwide
11 "Lord, have mercy" in Greek
14 Observe! Watch! See!
16 The essence of life God gave human beings
17 Literally "becoming flesh." God becoming a human being in Jesus of Nazareth
20 Anointed one, one set apart for a special task, Messiah
21 "So be it," a declaration of affirmation
22 (a) Praise to God, (b) "Praise God from whom" *Hymnal: A Worship Book* 118, 119
23 A statement of belief, for example, "I believe in God the Father Almighty . . ."
24 Pity, sympathy, kindness that is not deserved

DOWN

1   Change of heart, turning around
2   (a) A statement of belief and teachings, (b) admitting sin
4   Goodness and innocence, being in good relationship with God
5   Praise the Lord!
7   An image of Jesus as a sacrifice found in the New Testament
8   Separate, set apart
12 Timeless, never-ending
13 The death and resurrection of Jesus changing the relationship between humans, God and the world making us "at—one"
14 To ___ a person is to pronounce God's favour. To ___ God is to praise God and say God is good.
15 Leaner, student
18 One who rescues
19 If Jesus is the bridegroom the ___ is the bride.

Choosing Words for Worship

Scripture Text: _____

Worship Action: _____

Choosing words for worship

1. Scan collections of worship resources for texts that fit the theme of the service and function of the element. When you discover a text that may be appropriate, read it out loud to yourself and consider the following questions:
    *   Can you understand what is being said the first time you read the text? Do you know immediately and precisely what all the words mean?

        _____
        _____
        _____

    *   Does the text have a good rhythm? Is it awkward to read the text out loud?

        _____
        _____
        _____

2. Read the text again and consider the following questions:
    *   How does the text relate to the theme of the service? What words and phrases connect to the scripture reading and theme? How does it add? How does it distract? (consider central scripture readings, images, and ideas)

        _____
        _____
        _____

    *   How does the text fulfill its role in the service? Does it address God or the congregation? Which element does it fit? (Recognizing each other, recognizing God, blessing and commissioning)

        _____
        _____
        _____

    *   Imagine the congregation hearing or speaking the text. Is it an honest expression of the faith of the community? Would anyone feel alienated or hurt by the words? Does it use inclusive language for humanity and God? Review the comments on language for worship in Unit 4.

        _____
        _____

    *   What would you change about the resource? Could the text be used in combination with another worship resource?

        _____
        _____
        _____

Writing Opening and Closing Words Together

Module focus

How can we open and close worship in our congregation? Module 3 shows the group how to write opening and closing words for worship.

Leader preparation

Materials

- Scrabble™ game tiles
- Volleyballs or soccer balls (one per team)
- Masking tape
- 2 bowling pins or pylons
- Chalkboard and chalk *or* chart paper and markers
- Pens/pencils
- Music player, quiet instrumental music
- Visual focus with at least one candle
- Individual candles for youth
- Matches
- Sound maker*

Tasks

- *Opening activity*
  —Bring Scrabble™ tiles, volleyballs or soccer balls, masking tape, bowling pins or pylons. Set up for Scrabble™ bowling, as described in this section (p. 38), before the youth arrive.
- *Preparing for worship*
  —Reproduce the diagram in this section (p. 38) on chart paper or a chalkboard, and write down the two opening and two closing actions.
- Consider inviting a regular worship leader to work with the group for this module.
- After the module, print out the words for worship written by the youth. Schedule another time to rehearse presenting the words together. Consider adding *Unit 1 Module 3* (p. 21) as an additional module, to explore the role of the worship leader.

---

* See page 6 in the introduction for the suggested use of a distinctive sound and visual focus or worship centre for your *Reflection and prayer* time.

Session

Opening activity: Scrabble™ Bowling (10 minutes)

Warm up word skills with a round of Scrabble™ Bowling. Place three tables at one end of the room. On the centre table, arrange a set of Scrabble™ tiles, face down. Make a line with masking tape or rope at the opposite end of the room. Place two plastic bowling pins or small pylons several metres in front of the line near the tables. Each team requires a ball.

Divide the group into two teams. Each team chooses a speller to sit at their table. The rest of the team members line up behind the line and take turns rolling the ball to knock over the pin. The pin should be knocked over reasonably frequently (one-third to one-half the time), so adjust accordingly. A team member or leader stands behind each pin and sets it up when it gets knocked down.

When a player knocks over the pin, he or she runs to the end of the room, randomly selects a Scrabble™ tile, gives it to the speller and runs back to rejoin the line. The speller must spell a word with at least five letters. The first team to spell a valid word wins. (A different player can be the speller each round.)

Variation 1

Start by requiring a three-letter word and gradually increase the number of letters required each round, up to seven-letter words.

Variation 2

Teams are required to spell a word on a particular theme or topic. For example, a country, sport, type of tree, etc. Variation 2 is particularly useful if you are writing a call to worship for a thematic service.

Option

With fewer than six people, consider playing a party game such as Catchphrase, Taboo, or Boggle, or a simple game of Hangman instead.

Preparing for worship: Writing opening and closing words (25 minutes)

Teaching Moment: Worship is both a part of daily life and separate from daily life. The diagram shows how the opening words (vertical line on the left) and closing words (vertical line on the right) are a filter that allow some parts of everyday life to be unaffected by worship, others to enter into worship, and others to be left behind when we worship.

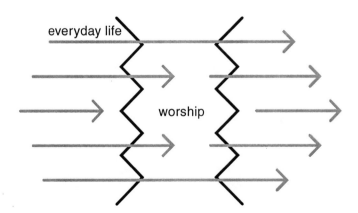

Two actions happen at the beginning of a service:
1. We recognize each other as a worshipping community
2. We recognize God's presence

Two actions happen at the end of a service:
1. Commissioning—we challenge the community to live as Christians in the world and take action based on the message of the service
2. Blessing—we extend the gift of God's peace, love and empowerment to others

Opening words take different forms:
- Responsive reading by leader(s) and congregation or parts of the congregation
- Reading presented by worship leader(s)
- Prayer directed toward God
- Words directed toward the congregation

Part 1: Personal reflection

Refer to the board or chart paper where you listed the two actions at the beginning and ending of a service. Give the youth time to reflect on these, thinking about how they relate to their worship experience.

Distribute the handout (p. 41). Ask youth to think about the questions and then complete the sentences (3 to 5 minutes). Give the following examples:
- Responses to the action, "We recognize one another as members of the gathered community of faith," could be: 1) We come with broken and painful relationships, and 2) We come to learn from Jesus and one another how to love all people, especially those we call enemies.
- Responses to the action, "We recognize God's presence," could be: 1) We come doubting our faith in God, and 2) We come expecting to meet God again and have our faith renewed.

Play music during the reflection time.

Part 2: Writing together

Divide the class into four small groups. Assign one of the four opening or closing actions to each group. They should combine their sentences into a single section of opening or closing words, using a consistent structure. For example, choose one of the following phrases that all groups must use to begin their section:

Examples:

O God, we come . . .   O God, we go . . .
Come as people . . .   Go as people . . .
Gather . . .   Leave . . .

Part 3: Revising together

Bring all groups back together and listen as each group shares their portion. Talk about how the pieces fit together, and whether anything needs to be changed.

Option:

Select a congregational response or refrain that everyone reads together.

Collect the texts written by the groups. Have someone take them home and type and print them. Schedule a time to rehearse prior to leading worship. *Note: An example of one application of this model can be found at the end of the session.*

Option

If your congregation does not use opening or closing words, write a prayer for a different point in the service, using this model.

Reflection and prayer (10 minutes)

It's important that the youth support each other with prayer. This will help strengthen their relationships and support them as they take on new responsibilities in worship. Gather around the visual focus and take a few minutes for each person to share a high point and a low point from the past week. If your group is large, break up into smaller groups for the sharing time.

Pass out the candles, one for each person. Begin with a time of silent prayer for each other with the usual sound. Light candles in turn, with each person naming the person on the right as they light the candle. When everyone's candle is lit, spend another minute in silence. End with a short prayer and the sound.

Example of opening words

All: **We come**
1: with highs and lows
2: good times and bad times
3: accomplishments and confessions

All: **We come**
4: with anxiety and stress
2: joy and happiness
5: exciting relationships and broken relationships

All: **We come**
3: to have our worry and grief lifted

All: **We come**
5: to grow closer to God
2: and to be part of the community

All: **We come**
4: to see friends
1: and share in one another's lives

All: **We come**
5: to talk to God
1: to feel relaxed
2: to learn
4: to worship and praise God

All: **We come!**

—Youth at First Mennonite Church, Kitchener, Ontario, October 2006

Beginnings and Endings

1. What thoughts, feelings, worries, excitements, etc., from everyday life do we bring with us to worship? Answer by completing the sentence:
    We come . . .

    _____
    _____
    _____
    _____
    _____

2. What do we hope to do or experience in worship? Answer by completing the sentence:
    We come . . .

    _____
    _____
    _____
    _____
    _____

Beginnings and Endings

1. What thoughts, feelings, worries, excitements, etc., from everyday life do we bring with us to worship? Answer by completing the sentence:
    We come . . .

    _____
    _____
    _____
    _____
    _____

2. What do we hope to do or experience in worship? Answer by completing the sentence:
    We come . . .

    _____
    _____
    _____
    _____
    _____

Youth Worship Leadership Suggestions

Getting creative

Open and close worship with more than words. How can the words used in worship be enacted physically? Examples:

- Remove shoes and place them at the front of the church at the beginning of the service and collect them at the end to recognize worship as creating holy ground.
- Mist the congregation with water to symbolize living water described in a call to worship.
- Smash a large glass jar to enact God shattering our expectations.
- Plant seeds at end of the service and watch them grow over the coming weeks to illuminate the parable of the Kingdom of God as a mustard seed.
- Start the service with a rainstorm of rubbed palms, snaps, claps, slaps and stomps, a group clap that gradually speeds up, or another action in which all can participate
- Set the tone for the service with a sound, such as an alarm clock, a bell, a hand drum rhythm, a singing bowl, or silence

How can the words be expressed visually? Examples:

- Assemble a display of objects as the opening words are read.
- Show a Power Point presentation with images relating to the theme of the service as the congregation enters the worship space.
- Ask each person to create a sculpture from modeling clay or a sketch of their response to the service which can be posted or placed on their way out as a blessing or commissioning.
- Write opening words based on a visual element such as a banner, display or projected image.

Use the gifts and experience of the youth:

- Begin the service with a thematic song of invitation, sung or played by a solo musician.
- Welcome the congregation in the many languages spoken by the youth.
- Lead the congregation out of the worship space with ballet dances as they are blessed to go with grace and joy.
- Bring produce from farms where youth live or work to create a display, if the theme employs agricultural imagery or thanksgiving.
- Ask youth who enjoy photography to take interesting and creative pictures of church members and create an artistic slideshow to use as a prelude and postlude.
- Start the service by having youth lead the congregation in a cheer, to express their enthusiasm about the work of God.
- Make a snack to encourage fellowship before or after the service.
- Ask several youth to share one sentence that gives their reason for being at church.
- Tell a story or perform a short drama to invite the congregation into worship.
- Use an idea borrowed from a summer camp where youth work or attend.
- Start the service with one of the elements the youth pick from the list in *Content for Learning and Teaching* (p. 25) from Module 1, or that they experienced in a different congregation. Try to find something that is less familiar to the congregation.

Ideas for closing the service as a large group

Having all the youth at the front of the worship space for the sending action can have a significant impact. There are many ways to make this possible:

- Use a sending resource that repeats the same line numerous times. This can be spoken by the entire group without notes, while individuals read lines in between. For example, "From where we are to where you need us," *Sing the Journey* 158.
- Give each youth the opportunity to add a word to a benediction. For example, on the theme "Images of God" the worship leader begins, "May the God who is . . ." and ends, "be with each one of you" while in the middle the youth say images of God that are meaningful to them.
- Choose one phrase, such as "The peace that passes understanding," that all the youth repeat at different times and speeds (and perhaps different locations in the worship space). Begin loudly and gradually decrease in volume until a signal is given and everyone whispers together audibly, "The peace that passes understanding be with you." Increasing volume is also a possibility, depending on the phrase, such as "Go and love," and mood of the service.
- Have all the youth extend their hands in a sign of blessing while the worship leaders speak the benediction.
- Sing a song of sending together as a group.

Youth worship leadership checklist: Opening and closing the service

Spiritual

1. Do the youth have the opportunity to pray together before the service?
2. Do the opening words open participants to each other?
3. Do the opening words open participants to God?
4. Does the opening make the purpose or theme of the gathering clear?
5. Does the opening welcome everyone (children, older adults, families, singles, people with disabilities, people of other races, cultures and languages, regulars, and visitors)?
6. Have you considered what the congregation will see, hear, smell, touch, taste, and feel when they enter and leave the worship space?
7. Does the sending provide an application of the theme of the service, provide assurance of God's blessing, and challenge participants to respond in their daily lives?
8. Do the youth have the opportunity to celebrate and evaluate the service several days later?

Logistical

1. Does everyone know where they need to be, what they need to have with them, and when they need to be ready for the service to start on time?
2. Do the individuals leading the opening words or actions know when it is time to begin?
3. Is all technology in place and fully functional, including visual and auditory equipment?
4. Do the beginning and end of the service flow smoothly into and out of what is before and after?

Music in Worship

Unit focus

Music is at the heart of worship. We sing to express and form our faith as individuals and a community. We carry songs and hymns with us on our lips and in our minds as we leave worship. Music is also a point of tension in some congregations. This unit:

* Emphasizes appreciating diverse styles of music in worship
* Considers the words and music we sing
* Presents a way of choosing music for worship that is based on something other than personal preference.

Unit 3 is accessible for both musicians and people who can't read music but enjoy listening and singing. In this unit, youth will choose and introduce music for a particular worship gathering. The words written by the youth in Module 2 can also be sung by the congregation in communal worship. Consider involving youth with musical training or experience in worship.

Each module can stand alone, or modules can be used in any combination appropriate for your group. Invite the music leaders in your congregation to be involved in the unit. Practical support is particularly valuable in Modules 3 and 4.

Unit outline

Content for Learning and Teaching
    Writing words for music
    Choosing music for worship
    Resources

Curriculum Modules
    Module 1: Appreciating Diversity
    Module 2: The Words We Sing
    Module 3: The Music We Sing
    Module 4: Choosing Music for Worship

Youth Worship Leadership Suggestions
    Leading music
    Getting creative
    Youth worship leadership checklist

Content for Learning and Teaching

Writing words for music

Hymn texts and song lyrics are poems set to music. Hymn texts often follow a certain metre (the number of syllables and the patterns of strong and weak syllables) and rhyming pattern. Other poetic devices, such as metaphor and alliteration, are also employed. Review the *Content for Learning and Teaching* in Units 2 and 4, especially on *Writing Words for Worship* (p. 64) and *Language for Worship* (p. 65).

Choosing music for worship

Three factors to take into account when choosing music for worship are:

1. Function within the service: What is the purpose of singing this particular hymn or song at this point in the service?

   Common functions:
   - Gathering—recognize God's presence, create a sense of community, prepare for worship, introduce the theme
   - Praise—praise God for who God is, give thanks for what God has done
   - Response—focus on the theme of worship, add to Scripture and sermon
   - Offering—offer time, talents, and resources to God
   - Sending—commission for life in the world, blessing

   Search strategies:
   - Uses in worship index
   - Table of contents
   - Browsing or flashes of inspiration

2. Thematic appropriateness: How does this hymn or song help the congregation reflect on and respond to the central ideas and themes of worship?

   Search strategies:
   - Scripture index
   - Thematic or topical indexes
   - Browsing or flashes of inspiration

3. Variety and balance: How do the hymns and songs fit together as a whole?
   - Musical style: international, spirituals, gospel songs, folk tunes, Taizé, contemporary, etc.
   - Text style: communal or individual focus, emotional or cognitive, concrete or abstract, simple or complex, etc.
   - Orientation: vertical (encounter with God), horizontal (engagement with community and self) and outward (empowerment for life in the world) movements of worship
   - Metre: speed and rhythm
   - Familiarity: familiar or new

Resources

Hymnals and songbooks

Hymnal: A Worship Book. Scottdale, PA: Mennonite Publishing House, 1992.

Hymnal Companion. Scottdale, PA: Mennonite Publishing House, 1996.

Iona Community resources available through Wild Goose Publications and GIA Publications. www.ionabooks.com

Sing the Journey. Hymnal: A Worship Book—Supplement I. Scottdale, PA: Faith & Life Resources, 2005.

Sing the Story. Hymnal: A Worship Book—Supplement II. Scottdale, PA: Faith & Life Resources, 2007

Taizé Community resources. www.taize.fr

Many praise and worship resources are available online.

Music and worship

Bell, John L. *The Singing Thing: A Case for Congregational Song*. Chicago: GIA Publications, 2000.

Bell, John L. *The Singing Thing Too: Enabling Congregations to Sing*. Chicago: GIA Publications, 2007.

Eskew, Harry and Hugh T. McElrath. *Sing with Understanding*. Nashville: Church Street Press, 1995.

Hymnal Companion. Scottdale, PA: Mennonite Publishing House, 1996.

Hull, Kenneth R. "Text, Music, and Meaning in Congregational Song." *The Hymn: A Journal of Congregational Song* 53.1 (2002): 14-25.

Kropf, Marlene and Kenneth Nafziger. *Singing: A Mennonite Voice*. Scottdale, PA: Herald Press, 2001.

Wren, Brian A. *Praying Twice: The Music and Words of Congregational Song*. Louisville: Westminster John Knox Press, 2000.

Appreciating Diversity

Module focus

What style of music is worship music? What are the strengths and weaknesses of different styles? This module explores the existence and value of different styles of music for worship.

Leader preparation

Materials

- Playlist or CD with diversity of spiritual music (see *Opening Activity*)
- Music player
- Copies of lyrics for two contrasting songs, one set for each participant (see *Discussion*, p. 48)
- Visual focus and sound maker*

Tasks

- *Opening activity*
  —Create a playlist or CD of praise and worship music and hymns, but also current secular and Christian popular songs, international music, Gregorian chant, bluegrass, classical, and music by local artists (including members of your congregation). Incorporate moods ranging from joyful celebration to painful lament. Include music familiar to the group and new music. If this is technically challenging, invite a youth to help out. Ensure one chair per person is available.
- *Small group discussion*
  —Print out the evaluation questions for comparing types of music on sheets of paper and post them.
- *Reflection and prayer*
  —Choose a song in a style unfamiliar in your context.

---

* See page 6 in the introduction for the suggested use of a distinctive sound and visual focus or worship centre for your *Reflection and prayer* time.

Session

Opening activity: Cooperative Musical Chairs (15 minutes)

Use the music mix to play cooperative musical chairs.

*   Begin with the same number of chairs as participants.
*   When the music stops (make sure it plays long enough to get a sense of the song), each person sits on a chair.
*   With each round, begin a new track and eliminate one chair. As the number of chairs decreases, the entire group must fit themselves onto fewer chairs without touching the ground.
*   Eventually the whole group must suspend themselves off the ground using as few chairs as possible.

Option 1

Play competitive musical chairs, in which there is always one less chair than person and both a chair and a participant are removed each round.

Option 2

With a smaller group, provide each youth or pair of youth with playing cards to build card castles or places of worship. Once every pair has used the cards to build a structure using all of the cards, deal more cards and switch to the next music track. Individuals or pairs must start over with each track. Consider arranging the tracks with increasing intensity. Deal cards so players are building with 2, 4, 5, 6, 8, 10, 12, 13, and 15 cards or more.

Discussion: comparing styles of music (20 minutes)

Small group discussion (15 minutes)

Play music in two different styles, such as an old hymn ("Be thou my vision," *HWB* 545), "All hail the power of Jesus' name," *HWB* 106, 285), a praise and worship song ("Here I am to worship" by Tim Hughes, or "Open the eyes of my heart" by Paul Baloche), or an international song ("Asithi," *HWB* 64, "Hamba nathi [Come, walk with us]," *STJ* 2 and Sing the Journey CD 1).

After playing both songs, divide the youth into three groups of three to four. (If you have more than 12 people in your class, two groups can focus on the same topic.) Distribute copies of the music (from a hymnal) or printed lyrics.

Assign the first group the topic "music," the second group "words," the third group "context." Explain that they have five minutes to evaluate the songs, using the questions for their topic. After five minutes, have them report back to the entire group. Allow time for responses at the end of each report.

Evaluation questions:

Music

1. What instruments are used?
2. How many people are singing? How many different notes are sung at the same time?
3. Is the rhythm steady and regular or varied?
4. Is the song hard or easy to sing?

Words

1. Approximately how many words are used?
2. Do the words rhyme?
3. Are parts of the song repeated?
4. Does the song use unusual words or phrases not used in everyday life? Are there words or phrases we do not understand?
5. Is the text focused on God or the experience of the singer?
6. Does the song focus on one simple idea or many complex ideas?
7. Is the song emotional (heart-centred) or cognitive (mind-centred)?

Context

1. Where would the song fit in a worship service?
2. Would this song be especially appropriate for a certain event (for example, baptism, Christmas, funeral, graduation)?
3. How old is the song?
4. Do you expect we will still sing this song in 75 years?

Large group discussion (5 minutes)

Discuss the following general questions with the entire group.

*   What are the strengths of worship songs?
*   What are the strengths of hymns?
*   Which style of music best helps you (personally) connect with God and others in worship and be empowered to serve the world? (Poll the group.)

Teaching moment: The music used in worship is diverse. Within one hymnal, we can find words and music borrowed from many cultures and collected over thousands of years. Certain styles are not more or less spiritual. It is important to respect the unique values and gifts each style of music offers and to appreciate how different styles help different people express their faith.

Reflection and prayer: Praying through music (10 minutes)

Place the visual focus in the centre of the room. Encourage each youth to find a personal space in the room to relax quietly. Begin and end a time of meditative prayer, accompanied by music, with the distinctive sound.

Consider using music less familiar in your context, such as choral music, praise and worship music, Gregorian chant, or music from the Taizé Community. If possible, provide a few words of introduction.

The Words We Sing

Module focus

What words are we singing? What are we really singing about? This module explores the words we sing in worship. It includes opportunities to analyze hymns and songs and to write new words for a simple song.

Leader preparation

Materials

- Hymnals, songbooks, and song lyrics
- Copy of the handout (p. 53) for each participant
- Paper
- Markers/crayons
- Visual focus and sound maker*
- Music player, instrumental music (see *Reflection and prayer*, p. 52)

Tasks

- *Opening activity*
  —Make a list of words for the Sing-Off. Use a combination of words common in church (Spirit, Jesus, pray, etc.) and words that are common to both secular and religious songs (peace, life, love, etc.).
- *Discussion*
  —Choose hymns or songs sung regularly in your congregation for small group discussion. Bring enough hymnals, songbooks and song lyrics for each person.
- *Preparation for Worship*
  —Learn the tune to the "Thank you" song (p. 51) and try writing your own lyrics according to the instructions, to familiarize yourself with the process.
- Invite a music leader to help teach the "Thank you" song and assist with writing lyrics.

* See page 6 in the introduction for the suggested use of a distinctive sound and visual focus or worship centre for your *Reflection and prayer* time.

Session

Opening activity: Sing-off (10 minutes)

The Sing-Off focuses the group's attention on carefully considering song lyrics.

- Divide the group into two teams.
- You will say a word, and the two teams alternate singing excerpts from songs that contain that word.
- They should keep thinking of songs until they run out of ideas.
- They cannot have longer than 10 seconds between songs.
- The first group that cannot think of any more songs that contain the word loses the round.

Option

With a small or quiet group, instead of singing the songs have each group write down as many songs on the theme as they can in two minutes. One point is awarded for each song not listed by anyone else.

Discussion: Hymn and song analysis (12 minutes)

Divide into pairs or groups of three and assign each group a hymn or song to analyze using the questions on the handout. Ensure enough hymnals, songbooks, and songs lyrics are available. Choose hymns or songs sung regularly in your congregation to encourage the youth to think more deeply about the meaning of the words they sing. After 5-7 minutes of discussion, ask each group to share select answers, including their one-sentence song summaries and any words or phrases that require explanation.

Preparing for worship: Writing words to sing together (18 minutes)

This activity gives the group an opportunity to write their own song for use in worship. They will use the simple tune GRACIAS, originally paired with the Spanish language text "Gracias por el amor," ("Thank you for love").

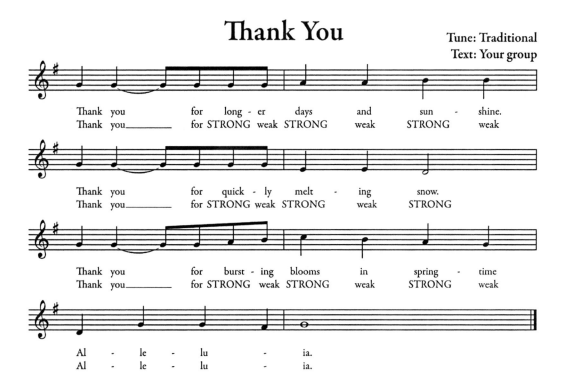

51

The song can be sung unaccompanied, with piano accompaniment, or led by a worship team. Each line begins with "Thank you for . . ." and each verse concludes "Alleluia" which means "Praise the Lord." The words to this song do not rhyme, but the number of syllables must correspond to each line and follow a pattern of strong and weak syllables:
Thank you for STRONG—weak—STRONG—weak—STRONG—weak.
Thank you for STRONG—weak—STRONG—weak—STRONG.
Thank you for STRONG—weak—STRONG—weak—STRONG—weak.
Alleluia.

For example
> Thank you for time to sing together.
> Thank you for voice and text and tune.
> Thank you for gifting us with music.
> Alleluia.

Directions:
- Begin by teaching this simple song by ear, line by line. Consider inviting a music leader from your congregation to help.
- After the group is familiar with the tune, explain the number of syllables and pattern of strong and weak syllables.
- Write the pattern down where everyone can see it.
- Divide into small groups. Instruct each group to choose a theme and write a verse for the song. *For example*, the theme of the following verse is spring:
  > Thank you for longer days and sunshine.
  > Thank you for quickly melting snow.
  > Thank you for bursting blooms in spring time.
  > Alleluia.
- Work with each group to ensure their text conforms to the pattern and there is variation among the themes of the verses.
- Gather the whole group and invite small groups to read or sing their verses.
- Compile the text for use in worship.

Reflection and prayer: The importance of music without words (5 minutes)

Module 2 emphasizes the importance of the words we sing. Music without words can also lead us in worship and prayer. Distribute paper and markers or crayons. Starting and ending with the distinctive sound, play instrumental music (not necessarily classical). Encourage the youth to listen to the music and reflect on it through colour and symbol, with recognizable pictures or abstract designs.

Hymn and Song Study

Read the words of the song aloud once, before reading and answering the questions.

Origin
1. When were the words written? Do you know anything about this time period?

    _____

    _____

2. Who wrote the words? What do you know about this person?

    _____

    _____

Content
1. Summarize each verse in one sentence. Avoid using words found in the song.

    _____

    _____

2. Summarize the entire song in one sentence.

    _____

    _____

3. What is the overall structure of the song? Does it have repeated sections? Does it have verses and a chorus?

    _____

    _____

4. What type of content is included? Does the song describe an impersonal truth or develop an idea? Does it describe a personal experience? Does it tell a story?

    _____

    _____

5. Is the song based on a specific Scripture passage?

    _____

    _____

6. Do any words or phrases require explanation? Are the ideas easy to understand? Why or why not?

    _____

    _____

7. What situations in your life does this text bring to mind?

    _____

    _____

Usage
1. On what occasions would it be appropriate to use this song?

    _____

    _____

2. This song would suit what age groups?

    _____

    _____

The Music We Sing

Module focus

How important is the tune we sing? How does the music change the meaning of the words? Module 3 explores these themes. It is an energetic session that works well with a large group.

Leader preparation

Materials

- Slips of paper with names of songs (enough for several per participant)
- Double-sided copy of the handout (p. 57) for each participant
- *Hymnal: A Worship Book*
- Chalkboard and chalk *or* chart paper and markers
- Visual focus and sound maker*
- Music player
- Recording of "Amazing Grace" (see *Reflection and Prayer*, p. 56)

Tasks

- *Opening activity*
  —Write the names of familiar songs on the slips of paper (nursery rhymes, children's songs, classical, oldies, popular songs, and familiar hymns and worship songs).
- *Discussion*
  —Invite a song leader, strong pianist, or other instrumentalist to join the group for the module and lead the different versions of "Amazing Grace." Provide the musician with the music in advance. If a pianist is available, make sure your meeting space has a piano or keyboard.
- *Reflection and prayer*
  —Find another version of "Amazing Grace" that is not familiar to your class or is not used in your congregation. Many recording artists have produced versions of this hymn (Elvis Presley, Destiny's Child, U2, Charlotte Church).

---

*   See page 6 in the introduction for the suggested use of a distinctive sound and visual focus or worship centre for your *Reflection and prayer* time.

Session

Opening activity: Name that Tune (15 minutes)

This game calls attention to the distinct qualities of different tunes. It encourages the group to become more comfortable singing together, in preparation for singing during the discussion.

- Divide the group into two teams.
- Have a player from one team stand. Give that person a slip of paper with a song name.
- The player must hum or "do-do" the song while the team members try to guess the name of the song.
- When they guess correctly, the singer moves on to the next song. The singer hums as many songs as possible in 30 seconds and receives one point for each song identified. One point is lost for every song that is passed.
- After 30 seconds, the other team is up.

Continue the game for 15 minutes. The team with the most points wins.

Option

With a group of fewer than eight, Name that Tune can be played individually, with one point going to the singer and one to the guesser for each correct match.

Discussion: The importance of tune (25 minutes)

Teaching Moment: "Amazing Grace," written by John Newton in 1779, is one of the most familiar hymn texts in North America. It is a musical autobiography of John Newton, a former atheist and slave trader, who converted to Christianity and later became an Anglican pastor and advocate for the abolition of slavery in England. This text is commonly paired with the tune NEW BRITAIN, as in Hymnal: A Worship Book (HWB) *143. Because many hymn texts are written in standard metres (with the same number of syllables and stresses on syllables in each line), they can be paired with many different tunes. "Amazing Grace" can be sung to a large number of tunes.*

With the help of a pianist, song leader, or instrumentalist, distribute *Handout 1*. Explain that you will sing the song "Amazing Grace" three times, to three different tunes. Begin with one or two verses to the usual tune, NEW BRITAIN.

Ask the group how they felt when they sang. Ask them to list words, images, or emotions they experienced. List the words on the board or on chart paper. You might need to start the list with one or two of your own responses.

Next, sing the first and last verses to the spirited tune, ANTIOCH, usually matched with "Joy to the World" (*HWB* 318). Make a second list of words, images, and emotions for this tune.

Finally, sing the first two verses to the less familiar THIRD TUNE, paired with "How shallow former shadows" (*HWB* 251). Repeat the question and make a third list for this tune.

Teaching moment: The music changes the meaning of the song. It influences which words are emphasized and our experience of singing the same words.

Divide into small groups and have each group prepare a version of "Amazing Grace" in the musical style of their choice and present it to the group. Expect hip hop, country, metal, electronica, rock, etc. Encourage the youth to think about emphasizing or repeating specific words or lines as is appropriate to their style.

Reflection and prayer: Praying through music (5 minutes)

Begin with the distinctive sound. Explain that you will play another version of "Amazing Grace." Ask the youth to listen for and reflect on what words and themes stand out for them on this particular day in their lives. End the time of musical prayer with the distinctive sound.

New Britain

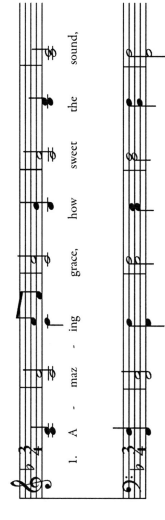

Example 1.

American folk melody, 19th century.
Harmonization by Edwin O. Excell, 1910.

NEW BRITAIN
8 6 8 6

Amazing grace, how sweet the sound,
That saved a wretch like me!
I once was lost, but now am found,
Was blind, but now I see.

'Twas grace that taught my heart to fear,
And grace my fears relieved;
How precious did that grace appear
The hour I first believed!

Through many dangers, toils and snares
I have already come;
'Tis grace has brought me safe thus far,
And grace will lead me home.

The Lord has promised good to me,
His word my hope secures;
He will my shield and portion be
As long as life endures.

Yes, when this flesh and heart shall fail,
And mortal life shall cease:
I shall possess, within the veil,
A life of joy and peace.

The earth shall soon dissolve like snow,
The sun forbear to shine;
But God, who called me here below,
Will be forever mine.

When we've been there ten thousand years,
Bright shining as the sun,
We've no less days to sing God's praise
Than when we'd first begun.

John Newton, 1779

ANTIOCH

THE THIRD TUNE

Example 2.

CM with repeat
ANTIOCH

Example 3.

CMD
THE THIRD TUNE

Tune by Lowell Mason 1836.

Tune by Thomas Tallis, The Whole Psalter
Translated into Englesh Metre, ca. 1567.

The material in this handout is in the public domain and may be photocopied.

Choosing Music for Worship

Module focus

How do we choose the music we use in worship? How can we introduce the music to the congregation in a meaningful way? Module 4 presents criteria for choosing music for worship that goes beyond personal preference. The youth will select music for a particular service and write introductions or prayers to accompany their selections.

Leader preparation

Materials

- Chalkboard and chalk *or* chart paper and markers
- Hymnals, songbooks, and other resources for congregational singing
- Visual focus and sound maker
- Paper with function and theme questions and search strategies from *Content for Learning and Teaching* (p. 45)

Tasks

- *Preparing for worship*
    - —Work with worship planners to prepare for the youth's contribution to a service.
    - —Determine the theme and Scripture text and the placement and purpose of music.
    - —Clarify how youth can contribute to music selection and song introductions.
    - —Write the following on chart paper or chalkboard: criteria for choosing music, theme and Scripture text of the service, and list of song locations.
- Invite a music leader from the congregation to serve as a consultant throughout the music selection process.

---

*   See page 6 in the introduction for the suggested use of a distinctive sound and visual focus or worship centre for your *Reflection and prayer* time.

Session

Opening activity: Prayer for inspiration (2 minutes)

Begin the module with a brief spontaneous prayer, inviting youth and leaders to be attentive to God's presence and inspiration as they prepare to lead worship. For example:

God, we thank you for the gift of music and the opportunity to lead our community in worship through music. Guide our conversations and musical choices. Amen.

Preparing for worship: Choosing music for worship (20 minutes)

Teaching moment:

1. *Briefly describe the criteria for choosing music for worship that goes beyond personal preference, included in the* Content for Learning and Teaching, *p 45. Make sure the function and theme questions and search strategies are posted in a visible location.*

2. *Explain the structure of the service for which the group will be selecting music. Where are the songs placed? Are they spread throughout the service or grouped together? What is the function of each song?*

3. *Explain the theme of the service. What is the central Scripture text? What theme will be emphasized by the speaker? Must special events or circumstances be taken into account?*

Small group discussion (10-15 minutes)

Divide the youth into small groups, based on the number of songs that must be chosen. Assign each group a particular location in the service (opening song, second song, closing song, etc). Ask each group to select three potential songs based on function and theme.

Provide the groups with resources, including any hymnals or songbooks used by your congregation and/or the resources used by a worship music team to select music. Encourage the groups to use the indices in the resources as well as draw on music they know.

Large group discussion

Gather the small groups and use a chalkboard to collect the proposed songs and hymns. Balance the selections according to musical style, textual style, orientation, and familiarity, as described in *Content for Learning and Teaching*. Finalize the musical selections so they are true to their functions and the theme of the service. Lead the group in making the decision through consensus, rather than voting.

Preparing for worship: Introducing music in worship (10 minutes)

Each group will write an introduction for the final song selection for their portion of the service. Even if songs are not usually introduced in your congregation, consider making an exception on this occasion.

- Explain that the introduction is several sentences spoken before the song is sung in worship.
- Give clear instructions about what must be included in an introduction in your context (for example, the title of the hymn and hymn number, instructions regarding standing or sitting, and musical directions).
- Suggest that the groups go beyond the basics to include a brief reflection on the purpose of singing the hymn, the topic of the hymn, a brief quotation from the text, a personal story connected to the hymn, or the story of how the hymn was written (for example, as described in *Hymnal Companion*).
- Practice introducing the songs to each other. For more discussion of public speaking, see the *Content for Learning and Teaching* (Unit 1, p. 8).

Option

If your congregation has a free-flowing, praise-and-worship music style, draw on themes and images in the texts to use in prayers, or find Scripture to read during instrumental interludes. Discuss possibilities with the worship music leaders.

Reflection and prayer: Choosing music for each other (13 minutes)

Gather the group around the visual focus. Pass out hymnals or songbooks, and ask the group to break into pairs. If you have an odd number of people, make one group of three.

Explain that each person in a pair will have two minutes to share a high point and low point from the past week. After the sharing time, they will choose a song that is relevant to their partner's life that week.

Begin with a short prayer. Allow five to seven minutes for the pairs to share quietly and then, in silence, choose songs for one another. At the end of the allotted time, invite the youth to tell their partners what song they chose and why.

Spend two to three minutes in silence, beginning and ending with the distinctive sound, as the group reads their songs. Then ask the youth to share what it was like to have a song chosen for them. End with a prayer song.

Youth Worship Leadership Suggestions

Leading music

- Consider forming a youth-led music team to lead congregational singing for one service or on a regular basis. Preparing music requires a significant time commitment and substantial musical training and organizational ability. Make sure that the team leader has appropriate musical skills and training. If there is no one in the youth group with these skills, ask an adult to lead the group.
- Invite musically talented youth within the group to share their gifts in leading music for the congregation, instrumental accompaniment for congregational singing, special music, or music before and after the service.
- Involve youth in operating sound or projection technology related to music.

Getting creative

- Ask if anyone in the youth group has written songs or plays in a band or group. If so, invite them to share the songs with you, one of the music or worship leaders, or the pastor. If the music is appropriate, considering using it during a worship time.
- Incorporate actions, dance, or visual elements into congregational singing. For example, accompany the hymn "I sing the mighty power of God" (*HWB* 36), or the worship song "God of wonders" by Marc Byrd and Steve Hindalong, with shifting visual images of the beauty of nature or the marvels of space.
- Begin the service with a drum circle that gradually builds from a single beat to a complex rhythm.
- Use *Module 2* (p. 50) to write a song together as a group to share with the congregation.
- Replace a song with an instrumental piece to create space for personal reflection.
- Distribute percussion instruments to children or adults for rhythmic songs.
- Integrate music into various elements of the service, such as prayer, preaching, time with children, Scripture reading, offering, gathering, or sending.

Youth worship leadership checklist: Music in worship

Spiritual
1. Do the youth have the opportunity to pray together before the service?
2. Has the music been carefully selected to lead the congregation in worship through particular functional and thematic roles?
3. Is the music balanced in terms of style, text, metre, orientation, and familiarity?
4. Do the youth have the opportunity to celebrate and evaluate the service several days later?

Logistical
1. Is it clear who will be introducing, leading, and accompanying music?
2. Are clear instructions given as to when and how members of the congregation can participate in the music (for example, by standing, sitting, singing in different languages, or clapping)?
3. Are the instruments and technical equipment for making music and projecting lyrics available, functional, and tuned?
4. Are all participants aware of where they need to be and what they need to have with them at each point in time?
5. Do individual songs and sets of music flow smoothly out of and into the preceding and following elements?
6. Is music selected for before and after the service?

Prayer

Unit focus

In worship, communities gather in God's presence to listen and speak to God. From one perspective, every aspect of worship is prayer. Many communities also identify prayer as certain moments in worship when individuals address words to God on behalf of the community, or when the community speaks to God with one voice.

Unit 4 explores different types of prayer present in worship, and the creative process of writing words for worship individually and corporately. The youth will lead the central prayer of the worship service, giving thanks and inviting God's action in the world, the community, the church, and the lives of individuals. The words written by pairs or individuals in Module 2 can be incorporated into worship, as well as the prayer written collaboratively in Module 3.

Each module can stand alone, but modules can be used in any combination. Invite a pastor or regular prayer leader to join the youth for this unit.

Unit outline

Content for Learning and Teaching
  Types of prayer
  The Lord's Prayer
  Writing words for worship
  Language for worship
  Structures for congregational prayers
  Resources

Curriculum Modules
  Module 1: Introduction to Prayer in Worship
  Module 2: The Creative Process
  Module 3: Leading Prayer Together

Youth Worship Leadership Suggestions
  Getting creative
  Youth worship leadership checklist

Content for Learning and Teaching

Types of prayer

Prayer is woven through worship. Short prayers are often included at different points in the service and serve different purposes. Common types of prayer in corporate worship are:

- Prayer of gathering/invocation
- Confession and reconciliation
- Congregational prayer/pastoral prayer/intercessions
- Prayers surrounding reading Scripture and preaching
- Offertory prayer
- Prayer of sending/blessing

The Lord's Prayer

The Lord's Prayer has been prayed around the world by many different types of Christians for the past two millennia. It is the one prayer used by all denominations of the Christian church. The Lord's Prayer is found twice in the Bible (Matthew 6:9-13 and Luke 11:2-4). There are many different versions of the Lord's Prayer. The following version is included in *Hymnal: A Worship Book*:

Our Father in heaven,
hallowed be your name,
your kingdom come,
your will be done,
on earth as in heaven.
Give us today our daily bread.
Forgive us our sins
    as we forgive those who sin against us.
Save us from the time of trial
    and deliver us from evil.
For the kingdom, the power, and the glory are yours
    now and forever. AMEN

Writing words for worship

Why should we write our own words for worship?

- To express and share personal experience, thoughts and feelings
- To add to the range of voices and perspectives heard in worship
- To speak to new issues
- To speak to old issues in new ways

Most worship resources available are written by adults, not youth. Resources written by youth offer a particularly unique and valuable contribution to worship.

The creative process

1. Begin with prayer: Approach the task with a contemplative and prayerful attitude.
2. Engage the imagination: Read the theme or Scripture. Note the thoughts, emotions, ideas, pictures, words, songs, etc., that come to your mind while you are reading.
3. Brainstorm: Write down options for developing the theme or text without evaluating or choosing between them.
4. Focus: Choose one idea as the focus. Base your choice on the needs of the congregation, the novelty of the idea, the possibility for developing the idea through other art forms, the importance of the focus in the context of scripture, or whether it is an issue that is often avoided and therefore may need to be addressed.
5. Let words flow: Allow ideas to flow freely from the focusing and brainstorming process, without worrying about perfection.
6. Take time away: Take a break. When you come back, you'll have a fresh perspective and possibly new ideas.
7. Revise: Consider the guidelines below about writing words for worship, and carefully revise the work with humility and open-mindedness.

Language for worship

- Simple and direct
  —Short, simple words and simple sentence structure are most effective.
  —Eliminate excess words.
  —Avoid using jargon or words just because they "sound religious."
- Concrete images
  —Use images from daily life.
  —Embrace diverse images and discover new images.
  —Appeal to all the senses.
  —Focus on one central image with other images to support it.
- Oral and rhythmic
  —Words are heard and spoken in worship.
  —Poetic language and words with fewer syllables are easier to read as a group.
  —Arrange texts with "sense lines" similar to the Psalms.
- Inclusive
  —Avoid using male terms to apply to all humans (mankind, brothers, etc.).
  —Do not reinforce prejudice against childhood, youth, age, singleness, race, or disability (for example, avoid language that associates blindness or darkness with sin, and sight and whiteness with salvation).
  —Use a wide range of images.
- Honest and biblical
  —Choose words than can be spoken honestly by the whole congregation, yet emerge from the deepest places of your experience.
  —Be reverent.
  —Integrate biblical images and stories.
- Correct and consistent
  —Use correct grammar, punctuation, and spelling to avoid distracting from the message.
  —Be consistent in type of language, whether formal or familiar. For instance, "Hey Jesus, we love thee" combines formal and familiar language.
  —Make clear transitions between addressing God and the congregation.
  —Proofread carefully.

Structures for congregational prayer

1. The ACTS acronym represents a structure for congregational prayer. Each element is addressed during the prayer time.

    A doration
    C onfession
    T hanksgiving
    S upplication

2. Intercessory prayer places individuals, communities, and events in the presence of God. It can be envisioned as concentric circles with prayers for the world, community, church, and individuals:

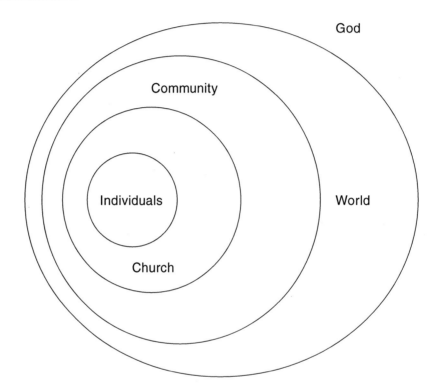

3. Formal intercession is a type of prayer where a leader or individual from within the congregation makes a series of brief statements concluding with a certain phrase and the community responds with another phrase. For example:

    One: For _____ we pray.
    All: Lord, hear our prayer.

4. Sharing time is an important part of congregational prayer in some communities. Individuals are invited to share joys and concerns in their lives, the congregation, community, and world. A leader or the congregation then prays spontaneously for what has been shared.

    All four models of prayer can be combined in different ways. For example, "supplication" may include prayer for all four circles of intercessory prayer, or each person who shares may conclude their statements with "we pray," to which the congregation responds, "Lord, hear our prayer."

Resources

Duck, Ruth C. *Finding Words for Worship: A Guide for Leaders*. Louisville: Westminster John Knox Press, 1995.

Hymnal: A Worship Book. Scottdale, PA: Mennonite Publishing House, 1992.

Mark, Arlene, M. *Words for Worship*. Scottdale: Herald Press, 1996.

Stookey, Laurence Hull. *Let the Whole Church Say Amen: A Guide for Those Who Pray in Public*. Nashville: Abingdon Press, 2001.

White, Julie Ellison. *Tent of Meeting: A 25-Day Adventure with God*. Scottdale, PA: Faith & Life Resources, 2004.

The Worship Sourcebook. Grand Rapids, Michigan: Baker Books, 2004.

Yoder, June Alliman, Marlene Kropf and Rebecca Slough. *Preparing Sunday Dinner: A Collaborative Approach to Worship and Preaching*. Scottdale, PA: Herald Press, 2005.

Zaerr Brenneman, Diane. *Words for Worship 2*. Scottdale, PA: Herald Press, 2009.

Introduction to Prayer in Worship

Module focus

What different types of prayer are practiced in public worship? What characterizes these types of prayer? This module explores the nature and purpose of different types of public prayer.

Leader Preparation

Materials

- Copy of the handout (p. 71) for each participant
- Pens/pencils
- Chalkboard and chalk *or* chart paper and markers
- Paper
- Worship resources (see list in *Content for Learning and Teaching*, Unit 2, p. 25)
- Copy of Lord's Prayer for each participant
- List of types of prayer for *Discussion* activity (p. 69)
- Recordings of your church services (optional: see *Discussion*)
- Visual focus and sound maker
- Music player
- Musical version of Lord's Prayer, shorter than 2 minutes (such as Steve Bell's "The Lord's Prayer")

Tasks

- *Opening Activity*
    —Fill in the gaps and copy the handout for each participant.
- *Discussion*
    —Familiarize yourself with the *Content for Learning and Teaching* (p. 64) on different types of prayer.
    —Determine whether your group will find example prayers or if you will provide them.
    —If you choose to play recordings of your church services, collect those.
    —Write the small group discussion questions on poster paper or a chalkboard.
- *Reflection and Prayer*
    —Make copies of the version of the Lord's Prayer used in your congregation.

---

*   See page 6 in the introduction for the suggested use of a distinctive sound and visual focus or worship centre for your *Reflection and prayer* time.

Session

Opening activity: Icebreaker Bingo (13 minutes)

Icebreaker Bingo identifies personal experiences that the group has in common and that are unique to each person.

- Give each person a copy of the handout and a pen or pencil.
- Each player gets others to sign up to a certain number of boxes. (For example—with 15 people, each person can sign up to two boxes; with eight people, each person can sign five boxes, or you can create a smaller grid.)
- The first person to have a signature in every box, or the player with the most signatures after 10 minutes, wins.

Teaching Moment: Public prayer in worship is different from praying on our own, because we are speaking for the whole community and placing the joys and concerns of the whole community in God's care. When we lead the congregation in prayer, we need to remember to be honest and express our own faith and experience. We also must recognize that we are speaking for others, and should be respectful and attentive to their faith and experience. For example, when leading a prayer of confession, we do not discuss our personal failings in detail, but rather confess in a way that reflects both our experiences and the experiences of others.

Discussion (20 minutes)

Divide the group into pairs or small groups to address the different types of prayer practiced in the worship service in your congregation. These may include gathering/invocation, confession and reconciliation, congregational prayer/pastoral prayer/intercessions, prayers surrounding reading scripture and preaching, prayer surrounding the offering, and sending/blessing prayer.

Assign each pair or small group one type of prayer from the list you created. Give them the descriptions of prayer from *Content for Learning and Teaching*.

Options

- With an older or more focused group, invite each pair or group to identify three prayers of the assigned type in the worship resources and analyze the prayers according to the questions below.
- With a younger or less focused group, choose prayers ahead of time and give each pair or small group three prayers to analyze.
- If prayer is always spontaneous in your congregation, listen to recordings of the service or ask a pastor to write down prayers similar to those used at different points in the service—three for each type of prayer.

Allow 12 minutes for groups to discuss the following questions:

1. What ideas or themes do the three prayers have in common?
2. What is different about the three prayers?
3. What do you think should be included in this type of prayer?
4. What is the purpose of this type of prayer?

Gather as a large group and invite each group to share their answers to the questions and, if time allows, provide an example of the type of prayer they analyzed.

Reflection and prayer (12 minutes)

Gather around the visual focus and distribute printed copies of the Lord's Prayer.

Teaching Moment: The Lord's Prayer has been prayed around the world by many different types of Christians for the past two millennia. It is the one prayer used by all denominations of the Christian church. The Lord's Prayer is found twice in the Bible (Matthew 6:9-13 and Luke 11:2-4). There are many different musical and spoken versions of the Lord's Prayer.

Begin with the distinctive sound, and pray the Lord's Prayer together. Have a leader pray it again very slowly, pausing after each phrase. Encourage the youth to reflect on the meaning of each line for them on this particular day.

Pause for one or two minutes, and then play the musical version of the Lord's Prayer. Invite each person to share the line that stood out or had the most meaning for them today.

Pray the prayer together again. End with the distinctive sound.

Icebreaker Bingo

Have broken a bone	Have played on a sports team	Have volunteered in the local community	Have seen _____ (recent movie)	Have voted in an election
Have travelled to five or more Canadian provinces or American states	Enjoy beautiful weather	Have applied for a job	Have never had chicken pox	Know the names of six neighbours on my street or in my building
Remember the death of a grandparent	Have four or more brothers and/or sisters	Have gifts to share	Have been in a wedding party	Have visited a baby in the hospital
Have written exams	Have travelled to the eastern hemisphere	Keep in touch with friends in another country	Participate in _____ (church program)	Read the newspaper/ online news regularly
Have been in a car accident	Have been to a church conference or convention	Remember the birth of a younger brother or sister	Have given money to a homeless person on the street	Have participated in a protest (march, rally, letter writing, etc.)

From *Youth Worship Source Book* © 2009 by Faith & Life Resources. Permission is granted to photocopy this page for use by one youth group using the *Source Book*.

Writing Words for Worship

Module focus

How do we write words for worship? This module presents Ruth Duck's creative process for writing short prayers called "collects." The prayers the youth write in this module can be used in worship.

It is helpful to write the steps of the creative process on a board or chart paper and uncover them as the module progresses. The nature of the creative process gives the Module a different shape than many others as it both begins and ends with prayer.

Leader preparation

Materials

- Chalkboard and chalk *or* chart paper and markers
- Music player and quiet music
- Candles
- Interesting visual centre (see *Opening Activity*)*
- Copies of the handout (p. 75)
- Sound maker*
- Bibles
- Paper
- Pens/pencils
- Familiar non-active game (see *Discussion: Preparation for Worship*, p. 73)

Tasks

- *Opening Activity*
  —Write the steps of *The Creative Process* from *Content for Learning and Teaching* (p. 64) on the board or chart paper and cover them with paper. Uncover each step as the module progresses.
  —Bring supplies to create a prayerful environment (music, candles, and an interesting visual centre) and set up before the youth arrive.
- *Discussion/Preparation for Worship*
  —Choose a Scripture text and theme.
  —Familiarize yourself with the "collect" structure for writing prayers. Write the structure on chart paper or a chalkboard where it is visible to all.
  —Familiarize yourself with *Language for Worship in Content for Learning and Teaching*. Write the list (titles only) in a visible location.

---

* See page 6 in the introduction for the suggested use of a distinctive sound and visual focus or worship centre for your *Reflection and prayer* time.

Session

Opening activity

1. *Beginning with prayer* (2 minutes)

    Before the youth arrive, create a contemplative atmosphere by dimming or turning off the lights, lighting candles, and playing quiet music. Provide an interesting visual centre to capture their attention, such as a piece of abstract art or sculpture, or an interesting object such as a lava lamp or unusual plant.

    Once the group has gathered, ask them to sit in silence. Make the distinctive sound and continue with at least one minute of silence. Say a short spoken prayer. For example:

    > *Creator God, we thank you for the many gifts you have given us that allow us to create alongside you: the inspiration of Scripture, the experiences that shape us, the advice of others, and the ability to use language and vivid imagination. Inspire our work today, as we prepare to lead our community in prayer. Amen.*

    Conclude with the distinctive sound.

Discussion: Preparation for worship (38 minutes)

2. *Engaging the Imagination* (5 minutes)

    Choose a Scripture text and theme to serve as the focus for reflection (see *Suggestions for Choosing a Scripture Text* in Unit 2, Module 2, p. 36). If your group is more mature, each individual could use a different text and theme, in which case the steps will be completed with greater independence. Otherwise, try using the same theme and text for the entire group.
    *   Encourage everyone to find a personal space in the room.
    *   Have two people read the text aloud.
    *   Read it once more yourself.
    *   Distribute handout, *Interacting with Scripture*, Bibles, and paper and pens for youth to record their thoughts.

3. *Brainstorming* (5 minutes)

    Gather as a large group and explain that you will go through a creative process together to write prayers to use in worship. Point to "The Creative Process," which you have posted.

    Brainstorm on the Scripture text using a "clustering" technique, writing the text in the middle of the board or chart paper and branching out from it on different themes. *For example*: with the theme "winter" in the centre, branches could include clusters of words about weather, winter sports, holidays, etc. Encourage the youth to call out ideas.

4. *Focusing* (3 minutes)

    Divide the group into pairs and ask each pair to choose one idea or theme from the cluster to explore further. Encourage pairs to choose different ideas.

5. *Letting words flow* (10 minutes)

    Teaching moment: There are many different ways to pray in public. Today we will use a traditional structure for writing prayers called "collects." These prayers have five parts, each about one sentence long.

73

Refer to the chart on the structure of prayer. Explain it and give an example, such as this prayer based on Matthew 7:7-8:

FIVE-PART STRUCTURE	EXAMPLE
1. Naming God	God who longs to be found,
2. Explaining what God does that makes the name appropriate	You have revealed yourself to us in the Exodus from Egypt and the coming of Jesus.
3. Makes a request of God	Give us the courage to search for you in new places,
4. Explains why the request is desired or what outcome is hoped for ("that" clause)	so that we can learn to live as your people today
5. Words of praise	in imitation of Jesus Christ the living Lord. Amen.

This structure is used not because it is the "only" or "correct" way to pray, but because it provides a starting point and a framework for exploring ideas. It can also be used as a guide for spontaneous prayers.

Give each pair time to prepare a first draft of their prayer.

6. *Taking time away* (10 minutes)
It is important to step back and focus on something else before revising. Take a break and play a favourite game that does not require a lot of teaching, such as a few rounds of Spoons or Catchphrase™, depending on the size of group. Avoid games that involve physical activity.

7. *Revising* (5 minutes)
Briefly explain the chart regarding the use of language in worship. Ask the pairs to revise their prayers based on the information in the chart.

Reflection and prayer (5 minutes)
Invite the group to gather around the visual focus and bring their prayers with them. Explain that they will read their prayers around the circle, after the distinctive sound and a few opening words.
Make the sound and open with a short prayer. For example:
God of many names,
We offer you our fragmented prayers:
Images, thankfulness, and requests woven together.
We offer you our words in response to your words to us in scripture.

Move around the circle, with pairs reading the prayers they wrote. Say "Amen" and end with the distinctive sound.

Collect the prayers and pass them on to a pastor or worship committee to be incorporated into worship. Invite the youth who wrote the prayer to pray it in the worship service.

Interacting with Scripture

Imagine yourself in the passage.

    What do you see? _____

    What do you hear? _____

    What do you smell? _____

    Can you taste anything? _____

    What is the temperature? _____

    What can you touch? _____

What experiences in your own life does the passage bring to mind?

    What places? _____

    What objects? _____

    What sounds, smells and tastes? _____

What image of God is revealed in the passage?

_____

_____

_____

What image of humanity is revealed?

_____

_____

_____

What questions does the passage raise?

_____

_____

_____

Which character do you identify with?

_____

_____

_____

Describe the relationships between the people in the passage.

_____

_____

_____

Writing a Prayer Together

Module focus

How can we lead our community in prayer? This module explores how to pray in public worship. The youth will prepare and lead a prayer in worship.

Leader preparation

Materials

- Chart paper and markers
- Chalkboard and chalk (optional)
- Paper
- Pens/pencils
- Bibles and worship resources
- Newspapers, church or community newsletters
- *Hymnal: A Worship Book* (optional)
- Visual focus and sound maker*

Tasks

- *Preparation for Worship*
  - —Familiarize yourself with *Structures for Congregational Prayer* in the *Content for Learning and Teaching* (p. 66).
  - —Choose one of the four structures or combine multiple structures as is appropriate in your congregation.
  - —Divide the chosen structure into 4 to 8 parts, based on the number of youth, so that a small group of 2 to 4 youth can work on each section.
  - —Write the structure on chart paper or a chalkboard where it is visible to all.
  - —Review the *Content for Learning and Teaching* on *Language for Worship* (p. 65). Write the list on paper or the chalkboard and post it in a visible location.
- Invite a pastor or regular prayer leader to join the group.

---

* See page 6 in the introduction for the suggested use of a distinctive sound and visual focus or worship centre for your *Reflection and prayer* time.

Session

Opening activity: Speed brainstorm (8 minutes)

Divide the group into two teams and provide each team with a sheet of chart paper and markers.

Give each team 4 minutes to list as many realistic prayer topics as possible. Encourage them to think of both joys and concerns and prayer for the world, local community, church and specific individuals. Suggest they attempt to remember previous prayers in your community.

When time is up, award one point for each original prayer topic (one not listed by the other team).

Preparation for worship: Writing a prayer together (25 minutes)

Explain the prayer structure you posted ahead of time. For example, you might have seven small groups prepare the following portions of the prayer:

1. Adoration
2. Confession
3. Thanksgiving
4. Supplication—world
5. Supplication—community
6. Supplication—church
7. Supplication—individuals/sharing time

Work with small groups to outline, write, and refine a brief paragraph appropriate for their portion of the prayer. Provide helpful resources, including Bibles, collections of worship resources, newspapers, and updates on members of the community. Review the Suggestions for Language in Worship from Module 2.

Consider the flow between parts of the prayer. It may be helpful to sing a simple song such as "O Lord, hear my prayer," by Jacques Berthier (*HWB* 348), or "Lord, listen to your children," by Ken Medema (*HWB* 353), between each section to ease the flow of ideas, people and writing styles.

There are many different ways to incorporate the elements from your prayer structure. For example:
*   Each group could prepare two formal intercessions on topics 3 through 7, and adoration and confession could be present elsewhere in the service.
*   One person or pair comfortable with spontaneous public prayer could prepare to lead a sharing time.

Practice praying the prayer together in the worship space at the conclusion of this module or before the service when the prayer will be used.

Reflection and prayer: Praying for each other (12 minutes)

Gather in a circle around the visual focus. If there are more than nine people, divide into smaller groups of five to ten participants. Ensure there is an adult leader in each group.

Invite each person to share a high point and low point from the past week. Each person should make a point to remember the high and low points of the person on their right.

Explain the prayer: Beginning with the distinctive sound, everyone prays simultaneously, out loud, for the person on their right. If anyone is uncomfortable praying, they can simply repeat the name of the person. If there is more than one group, all groups should start praying at the same time.

If it is appropriate and comfortable in your context, the group may hold hands or rest their right hands on each other's shoulders during the prayer. Continue praying for or repeating the name of the person until the prayer concludes with the distinctive sound. Spend a moment in silence and then repeat the sound.

Option

With a group of fewer than five, including adult leaders, consider praying for each person in turn.

Youth Worship Leadership Suggestions

Getting creative

- Add ritual to congregational prayer by inviting each participant to come forward and light a candle, place a stone, deposit a written prayer, or perform another action related to the theme and imagery of the service.
- Incorporate physical movement into prayer through kneeling, holding palms upwards, or walking a labyrinth.
- As is appropriate, include physical contact in prayer through holding hands, the laying on of hands, or hugging.
- Divide the congregation into small groups to share and pray for each other.
- Invite the entire congregation to pray aloud simultaneously.
- Incorporate music.
- Include a time for personal reflection.
- Practice silence, potentially beginning and ending with the distinctive sound.
- Pray using the repetitive music of the ecumenical Taizé community in France, some of which is included in *Hymnal: A Worship Book*. Each of these songs should be sung 10-15 times in a row.
- Use visual imagery (such as a slideshow) to lead prayer.
- Invite dancers to lead the congregation in prayer.

Youth worship leadership checklist: Prayer

Spiritual

1. Do the youth have the opportunity to pray together before the service?
2. Is the prayer authentic for leaders and inclusive of the whole congregation?
3. Does the prayer recognize both joys and concerns?
4. Does the prayer place both the church community and the world beyond in the presence of God?
5. Does the prayer use accessible and inclusive language and imagery?
6. Does the prayer reflect a biblical understanding and example of prayer?
7. Do the youth have the opportunity to celebrate and evaluate the service several days later?

Logistical

1. Do all leaders know where they should be, what they should be doing and what they need to have with them throughout the service?
2. Are the transitions between the different sections of prayer smooth?
3. Are the transitions between the prayer and the preceding and following elements of worship smooth?
4. Are other leaders involved in the service, including music leaders, sound technicians and sharing time ushers, aware of the youth contribution and their supportive roles?
5. Is the appropriate technological equipment functional, and are leaders aware of how to use it effectively?

Visuals

Unit focus

Worship engages the eyes, not only the ears and mouth. This unit addresses the role of visual elements in worship. It also creates an opportunity for youth to reflect on their experience of worship in different settings and identify key features of their experience of worship.

Youth will design and construct a lasting worship visual that will give them a long term presence in the worship space. Suggestions for creating a banner are included in the background information. Review this information before you begin. Expect the visual creation process to take longer than three sessions. Invite a member of your community with experience creating worship visuals to work with the group.

Each module can be used independently, or the three modules can be combined to begin the process of creating a visual. Consider using Unit 1, Module 3 (p. 21) to write a call to worship to accompany the visual.

Unit outline

Content for Learning and Teaching
Christian symbols
Designing and constructing a banner together
Adapting the banner project
Resources

Curriculum Modules
Module 1: Imaging Worship
Module 2: Images in Worship
Module 3: Designing Images for Worship

Youth Worship Leadership Suggestions
Getting creative
Youth worship leadership checklist

Content for Learning and Teaching

Christian symbols (descriptions on page 82)

1

2

3

4

5

6

7

8

9

10

11

12

13

14

15

16

17

18

19

20

Descriptions of Christian symbols:

1. Triquetra: early symbol of the Holy Trinity. The three equal arcs express eternity in their continuous form, indivisibility in their interweaving. The centre is a triangle, an ancient Trinity symbol.

2. Alpha and Omega: the first and last letters of the Greek alphabet, which signify that Jesus is the beginning and the end of all things (see Revelation 1:8).

3. Three-Step Cross: sometimes called the Graded Cross. The three steps, from the top down, stand for Faith, Hope, and Charity.

4. Fish: a secret sign used by the persecuted early Christians to designate themselves as believers in Jesus. The initial letters for the Greek words for "Jesus Christ, God's Son, Savior" spell the Greek word for fish (ICTHUS).

5. Shepherd: a symbol found in the Catacombs that calls to mind the loving care of Jesus, the Good Shepherd.

6. Latin Cross: the most commonly used form of cross.

7. Ship: the Church sails unharmed through all perils. The word "nave," used to describe the main part of some churches, comes from the Latin word for "ship."

8. All-Seeing Eye: the eye of God looks out from the triangle of the Trinity. It is found in some English and Greek churches.

9. Crown and Cross: symbolize the reward of life after death to those who believe in the crucified Savior (see Revelation 2:10).

10. Circle and Triangle: the eternity of the Trinity. The circle stands for eternity, because it is without beginning and without end. The equilateral triangle is the symbol of the Trinity. The three distinct angles combine to make one complete figure.

11. Fleur de Lis: a symbol of the Trinity; also represents Mary, mother of Jesus

12. Nimbus (halo): represents sanctity and a person recognized for unusual piety, such as apostles, martyrs, and saints.

13. Crown of Thorns and Nails: symbol of Jesus' passion.

14. I.N.R.I.: initial letters for Latin inscription on the cross: Jesus Nazarenus Rex Iudaeorum, "Jesus of Nazareth, King of the Jews." A symbol for Jesus.

15. Dove: a symbol for the Holy Spirit (Mark 1:10).

16. Bell: a calling to worship that symbolizes the priority for the things of God over the secular. In general, the sounding forth of the Word.

17. Candlestick: suggests Jesus' words, "I am the light of the world," John 8:12. They also represent Christ's two-fold nature, human and divine, when two candlesticks are used.

18. Bursting Pomegranate: a symbol of the resurrection and the power of Christ, who was able to burst the tomb and come forth.

19. Winged Creature with a Lion's Face: a symbol for Mark, because his Gospel narrative begins with, "the voice of one crying in the wilderness," which suggests the roar of a lion. Each of the gospels is associated with a winged figure: Matthew a human, Luke an ox, and John an eagle.

20. Five-Pointed Star: the Epiphany Star or Star of Jacob (Numbers 24:17). Finds fulfillment in the "manifestation" of Jesus to the Gentiles (Matthew 2:1, 2).

Designing and constructing a banner together

Tips before you begin

- Get help from someone who has experience making banners! This is a way for youth to get to know other members of the congregation. It will also make the whole process a lot easier if you involve someone who has made a banner before and is familiar with the process and materials.

- Choose the location where the banner will hang. Consider using a location where the banner can hang for longer than a week or two at a time. Measure the space in advance and determine what size and materials will work best.

- Make rough drafts and templates. Before handing the materials over to the youth, make sure they are ready to use them appropriately. Use materials that can be easily repaired or redone if a mistake is made—for example, cutting fabric, felt, or paper rather than painting or drawing.

- Banners can be expensive to produce. Find out how much funding is available and plan size and materials before starting to design the banner. Consider how long you would like the banners to last when choosing the materials.

- Provide a structure for the project, yet ensure that the youth rather than the leaders determine the content and images on the banner.

- Create a banner that is composed of a series of blocks, with each block presenting a specific theme. In this way, small groups can work on individual blocks rather than attempting to design and create a single image with a large group. Maintain consistent elements across blocks, such as colour and image size, to ensure that the blocks fit together as a cohesive whole.

- Questions to consider with the help of an experienced banner maker include:

Block Design
- —How many blocks will compose the banner?
- —How large will the blocks be?
- —Will the blocks be attached to a solid background, hang from one another, or be displayed separately?
- —How will the banner attach to the wall?
- —The ideal size for a small group is two to four, so the size of your group plays a significant role in determining the number of blocks. The blocks should be large enough to be visible from the back of the worship space, yet small enough to construct within a short period of time. Consider making two banners with two or three blocks each, instead of a single banner. Consider how the banners will fit in with other visuals in the worship space.

Materials
- —What medium will you use to make the banner?
- —Consider funds available, the desired lifespan of the banner, and artistic experience and ability of the youth and those in leadership. Paper and fabric allow for second chances more than paint. However, fabric may be expensive, and paper banners have short life spans. Purchase materials after the design stage to ensure that appropriate amounts are available. Cost and availability should be assessed prior to design.

Colours
- —How many colours will be used in the banner?
- —How will colours remain consistent across blocks designed by different groups?
- —Providing a limited number of colours helps create a sense of unity. Patterned paper or fabric may add texture and depth.

Example

In the fall of 2005, the youth at First Mennonite Church, Kitchener, produced a visual made of two banners, each composed of three 40-inch-square blocks. The panels hung from one another on dowels. The background of the banners was black, and the youth were given four colours of bright, subtly patterned fabric: red, yellow, blue, and green. The images designed by the youth were cut out of the coloured fabric and affixed to the black panels using iron-on webbing.

Option

With a small, committed group (fewer than four), it may be possible to integrate the youth into the earlier stages of the design process.

Adapting the banner project

- Instead of using the general theme of worship as described in the curriculum modules, the youth could produce a banner for a specific sermon series (using a central passage of Scripture or theme) or season (such as Lent or Advent).
- Adjust this project for different-sized groups by changing the number of panels or blocks in the banner. A small group (four or fewer) could make a banner with a single image and be more involved in the process (measuring the space, choosing the size, etc.). A large group could make a banner or multiple banners with six or more panels and would require a solid structure prepared in advance by the leaders.
- Many different materials can be used to create worship visuals (high quality coloured paper, fabric, paint, etc). Change the medium based on the artistic gifts of the youth and the congregation, the resources available, and whether or not the banner is intended to be a long-term investment.
- If a congregation objects to hanging banners in the sanctuary, explore the idea of visuals in worship through the creation of a slideshow presentation, a series of bulletin covers, or a hanging for another location in the church.

Resources

Krahn, Karmen and Leslie James. *Proclamation by Design: The Visual Arts in Worship.* Scottdale, PA: Faith & Life Resources, 2007.

Imaging Worship

Module focus

What are our experiences of worship? How do we define worship? How can we depict these ideas visually? This module explores how members of the group have experienced worship and how these experiences can be imaged.

Leader preparation

Materials

- Jigsaw puzzles *or* pictures cut into pieces
- Large sheets of paper *or* paper tablecloths
- Markers/crayons
- Copy of the handout (p. 88) for each small group
- Chalkboard and chalk *or* chart paper and markers
- Visual focus and sound maker*
- Small pieces of paper
- Pens/pencils
- Music player and music

Tasks

- *Opening activity*
  —Prepare cut-up pictures, portions from different puzzles, or sections from different areas of the same puzzle, each with the same number of pieces as the number of members in each small discussion group. (You may need to prepare several variations to adjust according to how many youth are present.) It is possible to leave all edges unfinished with "puzzle bumps," so that each puzzle can change size while still remaining a whole.
- *Discussion*
  —Cover tables with paper or paper tablecloths. Put a set of markers or crayons at each table
- *Reflection and prayer*
  —Provide music such as *Heart of Worship*—Matt Redman; *Here I am to Worship*—Tim Hughes; *Sanctuary*—John W. Thompson, Randy Scruggs; "Be thou my vision"— *HWB* 545.
- Consider inviting other adult leaders who will assist with the banner.

---

*   See page 6 in the introduction for the suggested use of a distinctive sound and visual focus or worship centre for your *Reflection and prayer* time.

Session

Opening activity: Puzzle piece game (5 minutes)

This game randomly divides a large group into small discussion groups. Have participants draw a puzzle piece from a hat. When you give the sign, each person must find the others who have pieces that fit with theirs. The first group to complete their puzzle wins.

Option

This game works best with a group of 12 or more youth, dividing into groups of three or four people. With a smaller group, the session could start with having pairs or groups of three or four race to finish two puzzles of similar difficulty. This would also be an easier way to integrate youth who arrive throughout the first portion of the session.

Teaching moment: Many different pieces combine to create worship. Each person has a different experience of worship. Everyone's piece is necessary for understanding what worship is all about.

Discussion/preparation for worship:
Experiencing and defining worship (25 minutes)

Small group discussion

Use the groups from the *Opening Activity*. Have each group gather around a table covered with paper and equipped with markers or crayons. Instruct them to discuss and illustrate answers to the questions on *Handout 1*, as a first step toward creating a banner.

Gather and discuss these questions as a large group, with the drawings displayed:

- What types of worship gatherings did you list?
- What did your worshipful experiences have in common?
- What different elements of worship arose from your discussions?
- What were your four key words? (For example: Bible, community, energy, music) Use the key words to create a master list. Note repetitions and themes.

Teaching moment: Four parts of worship that have been important to Christians around the world since the beginning of the church are: 1) reading the Bible, 2) sharing the Lord's Supper, 3) baptism, 4) attending to the needs of the poor. Question: Were these four items on our lists? Why or why not?

Option

If you are using a different theme for the banner, you may instead wish to spend the first session discussing your theme. This format can also be used to discuss worship without the eventual goal of producing a banner.

Reflection and prayer (15 minutes)

Teaching moment: Worship is not just something we do on Sunday morning. It is a way of life.

Gather around the visual focus and place the list of key words about worship in a visible location. Distribute pens or pencils and small pieces of paper.

Ask the youth to illustrate how we can use three of the elements of worship you discussed to worship God in everyday life. For example, a drawing of two friends hugging could represent the worship element "community," showing how supporting a friend going through a difficult time can be a form of worship.

Begin with the distinctive sound and start the music. Encourage everyone to find a personal space in the room and spend time in quiet reflection.

After three minutes, make the sound and gather the group back together. Ask them to silently bring their papers and place them near the visual focus as an offering to God. Close with a short prayer, such as:

Our God, When we gather to worship you on Sunday morning it is set apart as a sacred time, but our worship extends beyond that hour to our everyday lives. We offer you our worship as we try to understand you and follow you in every situation we encounter each day. Amen.

Imaging Our Worship Experiences

1. What different types of worship gatherings can you think of? For example, Sunday service at church, campfire, funeral, etc. Draw images or symbols that represent these times of worship.

2. When and where have you had worshipful experiences? Draw, describe, and share one experience with your small group.

3. What elements are involved in worship? What elements were involved in your experience? Did these help make your experience meaningful? If yes, explain how. If no, explain why not. Add symbols, images, and words to your images.

4. What essential elements define worship? Write down four words or elements that define worship for your group. Illustrate.

Imaging Our Worship Experiences

1. What different types of worship gatherings can you think of? For example, Sunday service at church, campfire, funeral, etc. Draw images or symbols that represent these times of worship.

2. When and where have you had worshipful experiences? Draw, describe, and share one experience with your small group.

3. What elements are involved in worship? What elements were involved in your experience? Did these help make your experience meaningful? If yes, explain how. If no, explain why not. Add symbols, images, and words to your images.

4. What essential elements define worship? Write down four words or elements that define worship for your group. Illustrate.

Images in Worship

Module focus

How can we connect with God through art and symbolism? This module explores how visual images can help us connect with God.

Leader preparation

Materials

- Magic Eye posters (see *Opening activity*)
- 4 or more large visual images (see *Discussion*, p. 90)
- Copy of the handout (p. 92) for each small group
- Pens/pencils
- Visual focus and sound maker
- Music player, quiet instrumental or choral music

Tasks

- *Discussion*
  —Find large visual images.

---

* See page 6 in the introduction for the suggested use of a distinctive sound and visual focus or worship centre for your *Reflection and prayer* time.

Session

Opening activity: Magic Eye (5 minutes)

Magic Eye is the type of image that initially appears to be simply a pattern, but after several seconds a three-dimensional image stands out. If possible, make sure there are enough of these images to have no more than two people per image. Youth can spend a few minutes trying to see the Magic Eye images.

Option:

If it is not possible to obtain Magic Eye images, use optical illusions.

Teaching Moment: Sometimes after looking at an image for a while, we begin to see it differently and notice new ideas and meanings.

Discussion: Experiencing God in different art forms (30 minutes)

Small group discussion

Divide into small groups to discuss different pieces of art. Use at least four different images, to convey the idea that we can understand God through many different art forms and styles. Five possibilities are:

1. Rembrandt—Return of the Prodigal Son

   The well known theologian Henri Nouwen wrote *The Return of the Prodigal Son*, a book based on Rembrandt's painting and its impact on his own life of faith.

2. Kandinsky—Harmonie Tranquille (or another abstract piece by Kandinsky)

   Kandinsky understood his abstract work to be spiritual. It is an example of how we can find images of God even where they are not explicit or obvious.

3. Collection of traditional Christian symbols from *Content for Teaching and Learning* (p. 81)

   Symbols associated with Christianity permeate our churches and our culture so much that we rarely take time to consider their meanings.

4. Stained glass depicting Scripture verses or characters from the Bible

   Stained glass images served as teaching tools in an illiterate society and therefore contain complex symbolism about people and stories of faith.

5. Banner commonly used in the sanctuary

   In our own churches we have many beautiful artistic expressions of the divine. We do not need to look to great artists or traditional symbols.

Ideally, find large posters of each image. If this is not possible, find the images online or in library books. Provide each group with a different image and the handout. Inform them they will be expected to share their responses with the larger group.

When a group has answered the questions, provide them with more detailed information about the image, artist, and meaning of the work.

Large group discussion

Gather as a large group and have each small group share the results of their conversation. Pose an additional question about each image for general discussion after each group shares their findings:

- Rembrandt—With which figure do you identify most? (vote)
- Kandinsky—How could this image represent God? Where is God in this image?
- Symbols—Which symbol reflects where you are with your faith today? (vote)
- Stained Glass—What story does this stained glass tell?
- Banner—Why do we use this image in worship at our church?
- With which image do you identify most? (vote)

Option

Small groups of three or four people per image are ideal. You can have more than one group discuss an image, if you have a large group. If your class is small, have the entire group discuss all images.

Reflection and prayer (10 minutes)

Gather around the visual focus and explain the time of reflection. Invite each person to sit so they can see the image that is most interesting or meaningful to them. Ask them to think about the following questions:

How does this image represent God for you?

Where do you see God in this image?

Make the distinctive sound and start the music. Allow 10 minutes of quiet time. Make the distinctive sound and close with prayer. For example:

Many-imaged God, We thank you for revealing yourself to us in so many ways:

Through the gifts of great artists

Through symbols and stories, and

Through the art of members of our own congregation.

Help us to look for you and to expect to encounter you

in the images of our worship and our lives. Amen.

Encountering Images

1. What is your initial reaction to the image?
   _____
   _____
   _____

   —Do you like it? _____

   —What words first come to mind? _____

   —Have you ever seen it before? _____

2. What is happening?
   _____
   _____
   _____

   —What is the subject of the image? _____

   —Is there action? What is the action?
   _____

   —Are there any words or letters? What do they mean?
   _____

3. What does the image mean? Where do you see God in the image?
   _____
   _____
   _____

   —Is there anything obviously religious? _____

   —Is there anything you can interpret as having religious meaning?
   _____

4. How is this image related to worship?
   _____
   _____

   —How could it be used in worship?
   _____
   _____

Designing Images for Worship

Module focus

What are the key ideas in our understanding of worship, and how can we represent these ideas visually? This module begins the process of designing a worship visual as a group. Expect the creation of the visual to take two to four additional sessions.

Leader preparation

Materials

- Paper
- Markers, pencils, crayons
- Copy of the handout (p. 96) for each participant
- Images and lists of key worship words from Unit 5, Module 1 (p. 86)
- Visual images used in Module 2 (p. 90)
- Chalkboard *or* whiteboard (optional)
- Visual focus and sound maker*

Tasks

- *Opening activity*
    —Create a list of the essential elements of worship gathered in *Module 1* (p. 86)
    —Add any other appropriate words, to make a total of 12-17 words (for example, *Jesus, energy, Scripture, community,* or *worship elements, actions,* and *movements* from Unit 1 [p. 9]).
    —Make two stacks of paper with the same number of sheets as words on the list and each page clearly numbered.
    —Provide markers for two teams.
- *Preparation for worship*
    —Review Designing and *Constructing a Banner Together* in *Content for Teaching and Learning* (p. 83)
    —Create a banner framework for your group, with the help of an experienced worship visual creator.
- Consider inviting other adult leaders who will assist with the banner.

---

* See page 6 in the introduction for the suggested use of a distinctive sound and visual focus or worship centre for your *Reflection and prayer* time.

Session

Opening activity: Pictionary Relay (15 minutes)

This game gets youth thinking about how to represent words relating to worship with simple images.

- Divide the group into two teams.
- Have the teams move as far apart as possible within the space, while remaining the same distance from the leader, who has the list of words.
- One team member at a time runs to the leader, who hands the person a word.
- The player returns to the team and then draws images and symbols to get the rest of the team to guess the word. The "drawer" cannot use letters, numbers, spoken words, physical actions, or indicate the number of letters or words in any way.
- When the team guesses the word, the next team member runs to get the next word on the list.
- All team members must draw before anyone draws for a second time. The first team to finish the entire list of words wins.

Option

With a small group, individuals can take turns drawing while the rest of the group guesses.

Preparation for worship: Banner design (25 minutes)

Prepare to discuss banner design

This is where it all comes together. The discussions from Module 1 and Module 2 are transformed into the banner design and production process. In order for this process to occur with ease, you must have some guidelines in place. It is important to allow as much room for creativity from the youth as possible, while at the same time creating clear boundaries to ensure a usable finished product.

Large group banner design

- Gather as a large group and quickly review the past two sessions.
- Post the list of *Essential Elements of Worship* from Module 1 (p. 9), the images discussed in Module 2 (p. 89), and drawings from the Pictionary game in this module's opening activity.
- As a group, discuss which key words you would like to represent on the banner. The number of words chosen should correspond to the number of blocks. A chalkboard or whiteboard may be helpful in this conversation. Questions to consider:
  —Should any words/ideas on the list obviously not be included?
  —Should any words/ideas on the list obviously be included?
  —Is anything missing that should be on the list?
  —How do these ideas fit together as a whole?
- Discuss until the group reaches consensus on the theme for each block.

Small group block design

- Explain the limitations on the banner design, including the size of the blocks, colours available, and timeline.
- Divide the youth into small groups to begin brainstorming ideas for each block theme. These small groups will continue to work together on the same block for following sessions, so take special care to form balanced groups that work well together.
- Provide each group with paper, pencils, markers or crayons, and encourage them to sketch anything that comes to mind in relation to their theme.
- In the following sessions, have youth create the templates and the final product. Consider writing a call to worship based on the banner using the model in Unit 2, Module 3 (p. 38).

Reflection and prayer (5 minutes)

Invite God into the creative process through reading a litany. Gather around the visual focus and distribute copies of the handout. Invite the youth to read over the litany individually before reading together. Begin and end the reading with the distinctive sound.

Prayer for Creative Guidance

Leader: Creator God,
You call us to be co-creators with you.

All: ***Inspire us,***

Female: Through stories of your presence in Scripture,

Male: Through experiences of you in our lives,

Female: Through conversation with one another.

All: ***Guide us,***

Male: In sketching images that express our thoughts of you,

Female: In making shapes that express our feelings towards you,

Male: In choosing colours that express our worship of you.

All: ***Be present with us,***

Female: As we offer our individual gifts and abilities,

Male: As we form a whole that is more than the sum of its parts,

Female: As we prepare to lead our friends and families in worship.

Leader: We ask that your Spirit be present with us at this time, in this place, as we prepare to lead in the worship of you, who are beyond both time and space. Amen.

From *Youth Worship Source Book* © 2009 by Faith & Life Resources. Permission is granted to photocopy this page for use by one youth group using the *Source Book.*

Prayer for Creative Guidance

Leader: Creator God,
You call us to be co-creators with you.

All: ***Inspire us,***

Female: Through stories of your presence in Scripture,

Male: Through experiences of you in our lives,

Female: Through conversation with one another.

All: ***Guide us,***

Male: In sketching images that express our thoughts of you,

Female: In making shapes that express our feelings towards you,

Male: In choosing colours that express our worship of you.

All: ***Be present with us,***

Female: As we offer our individual gifts and abilities,

Male: As we form a whole that is more than the sum of its parts,

Female: As we prepare to lead our friends and families in worship.

Leader: We ask that your Spirit be present with us at this time, in this place, as we prepare to lead in the worship of you, who are beyond both time and space. Amen.

From *Youth Worship Source Book* © 2009 by Faith & Life Resources. Permission is granted to photocopy this page for use by one youth group using the *Source Book.*

Youth Worship Leadership Suggestions

Getting creative

- Introduce the theme of a service with a visual display outside the worship space, where people enter the building.
- Assemble a visual display or image during the service.
- Use data projection to display still or moving images.
- Make a video or slideshow of images relating to the theme and show it before and after the service.
- Work in three dimensions with fabric, symbol, or sculpture.
- Invite one or two artistic youth to design a bulletin cover or series of bulletin covers.
- Invite an artistic youth to work with a preacher to draw or paint in response to the sermon as it is preached.
- Decorate the worship space for a season of the church year, such as Advent or Lent, or a particular day, such as Epiphany or Pentecost.
- Reflect on how the semi-permanent visuals in the worship space, including plants and furniture, could be rearranged for a certain service, series or season.

Youth worship leadership checklist: Visuals

Spiritual

1. Do the youth have the opportunity to pray together before the service?
2. Is adequate explanation provided for the congregation regarding the meaning of the visuals?
3. Is it clear to the congregation (in the bulletin and announced during the service) that the youth designed and created the worship visuals?
4. Do the youth have the opportunity to celebrate and evaluate the service several days later?

Logistical

1. When and how will the banners be hung?
2. Who is responsible for the storage, cleaning, and maintenance of the banners?
3. Is all technical equipment functioning correctly?

Scripture

Unit focus

Scripture—proclaiming, hearing, and responding to God's story—is at the centre of worship. Scripture is the starting point for planning and leading worship. The stories and language of the Bible can be part of every aspect of worship. This unit explores different ways of choosing the Biblical texts that are the basis for worship, how Scripture can be integrated into every aspect of worship, how to read and listen to Scripture, and how to present Scripture creatively.

Youth will present one or more Scripture texts during Sunday morning worship. The unit will teach youth how to read Scripture well, so that individual youth or small groups can be invited to read Scripture on a regular basis.

Before beginning this unit, find out what Scriptures will be used on the Sunday the youth are leading worship.

Each module can stand alone, but modules can be used in any combination. Use the modules that are most appropriate in your context.

Unit outline

Content for Learning and Teaching
    Choosing Scripture
    Reading Scripture
    Resources

Curriculum Modules
    Module 1: Introduction to Scripture in Worship
    Module 2: Reading and Listening to Scripture in Worship
    Module 3: Creatively Presenting Scripture in Worship Together

Youth Worship Leadership Suggestions
    Leading Scripture
    Youth worship leadership checklist

Content for Learning and Teaching

Choosing Scripture

Various methods are used to determine the Scripture used for worship. Three common approaches are:

1. *Lectionary*: A lectionary is a schedule of Scripture readings arranged and intended for proclamation during corporate worship. For example, the Revised Common Lectionary is a three-year schedule commonly used in North American churches, including Mennonite churches. Four Scripture readings are provided for each Sunday: an Old Testament reading, a psalm, a reading from one of the epistles, and a gospel reading. At least one reading from each book of the Bible is included over the three-year cycle. A lectionary is a disciplined approach to covering a wide range of Scripture.

2. *Theme*: Scripture readings are chosen based on the theme of a single worship service or a series of services. For example, a series of services could address stewardship or the parables of Jesus. A thematic approach allows congregations to focus on contemporary issues.

3. *Book study*: A single book of Scripture may serve as the basis for a series of worship services. For example, a congregation could structure a series of five to ten services around the book of James. Book study permits in-depth reflection on a larger portion of Scripture.

Mennonite churches use different approaches to choose Scripture for worship. They often use a combination of the three approaches described above. Seasonal worship resources for the seasons of Advent, Lent, and Easter, prepared by the Mennonite Church, are often based on the lectionary.

Reading Scripture

Reading Scripture should be the high point of worship. Unfortunately, many congregations do not pay adequate attention to Scripture reading or devote time and teaching to nurture effective Scripture readers. Reading Scripture is always interpreting Scripture, and must receive the attention worthy of this task. Scripture readers are called to elevate the message of Scripture; to get themselves out of the way, so that the word of God can come alive for the congregation. Scripture readers can use the following guidelines to be more effective:

Preparing to read Scripture

1. Read the text and make sure you understand its meaning. If you don't understand the text, the congregation won't understand it.
2. Choose what translation of the Bible you will use. Check to see if a specific version is used in your congregation. If you want to use a different version, clear it with someone.
3. Consider printing out a copy of the passage in larger print, with double spacing, to make it easier to read.
4. Mark pauses and words you wish to emphasize.
5. Plan how you will introduce the text. For example, "A reading from the gospel according to Matthew, Chapter 5."

6. Use proper names for people who were introduced earlier in the chapter or book. You can also give a short description, or set the scene, when you introduce the passage. For example: Paul sent this message to the Corinthian church. In this passage, he is talking to the leaders of the church.

7. Plan how to conclude the text. For example, certain congregations conclude Scripture readings with a phrase such as, "This is the Word of the Lord. Thanks be to God!"

8. Read through the text several times ALOUD before reading it during the worship service.

9. Record yourself at least once, so you can hear how you sound.

10. Read the passage for others and ask them for feedback.

Tips for reading Scripture

- *Speed*: Read slowly. Add pauses in appropriate places.
- *Tone*: Clearly begin and end each sentence. Avoid raising your voice in a "question" at the end of a sentence, or allowing it to drop off at the end of a phrase.
- *Form*: The Bible includes history, story, prophecy, poetry, song, teaching, and law, among other forms of material. Read a passage of Scripture in a manner appropriate to its form. For example, tell a story, rather than simply reading it.
- *Content*: The Bible reflects many different thoughts and emotions. Read a passage in a way that reflects its content. For example, read a description of the crucifixion sorrowfully, and an account of the resurrection joyfully.
- *Posture, gestures, and eye contact*: Stand still and keep your hands still. Consider placing your hands on the lectern. Memorize how you will introduce the reading and look at the congregation as you make the introduction. Feel free to look at the text rather than the congregation while you read. Memorize the final phrase of the passage and look up again at the end.
- *Listen*: Listen to yourself reading the Scripture text. Focus on the message, not on your technique or the audience.
- *Engage*: Be responsive to what the passage is saying to you. Let the text come to life in you. Let the text bring you to life. Let it show!

Resources

The Lectionary

Mennonite Church USA. "Lectionary."
www.mennoniteusa.org/Home/Leaders/Lectionary/tabid/203/Default.aspx

"The Revised Common Lectionary." http://divinity.library.vanderbilt.edu/lectionary/

The Worship Sourcebook. Grand Rapids: Baker Books, 2004.

Integrating Scripture into each element of worship

Kreider, Eleanor. *Enter His Gates.* Scottdale, PA: Herald Press, 1990.

Mark, Arlene. *Words for Worship.* Scottdale, PA: Herald Press, 1996.

The Worship Sourcebook. Grand Rapids: Baker Books, 2004.

Check the Scripture index in worship resources.

Reading Scripture aloud

"Common Translations of the Bible." *The Mennonite Handbook.* Scottdale, PA: Herald Press, 2007, p. 126.

Jacks, G. Robert. *Getting the Word Across: Speech Communication for Pastors and Lay Leaders.* Grand Rapids: William B. Eerdmans, 1995.

Yoder, June Alliman, Marlene Kropf and Rebecca Slough. *Preparing Sunday Dinner: A Collaborative Approach to Worship and Preaching.* Scottdale, PA: Herald Press, 2005.

Scripture dramas for youth

Bell, John L. and Graham Maule. *Jesus and Peter: Off-the-Record Conversations.* Chicago: GIA Publications, 1999.

Morton, Craig and Ken Hawkley. *Word of Mouth: Creative Ways to Present Scripture.* Scottdale, PA: Herald Press, 2000.

Shelley, Patricia J. *Let All Within Us Praise! Dramatic Resources for Worship.* Newton: Faith & Life Press, 1996.

Devotional use of Scripture

White Julie Ellison. *Tent of Meeting: A 25-Day Adventure with God.* Scottdale, PA: Faith & Life Resources, 2004.

Introduction to Scripture in Worship

Module focus

How are specific pieces of Scripture chosen for worship? How is Scripture incorporated into every element of worship? This module explores the use of Scripture as the foundation for worship planning. If time is limited, consider using only Part 1 or Part 2 of the discussion, as is most relevant in your context.

Leader preparation

Materials

- Copies of the handout (p. 105), enough for half your group; note that it is two pages, and it should be copied back to back
- Bibles
- Pens/pencils
- Chalkboard and chalk *or* chart paper and markers
- 2 sheets of paper, one labelled "Most Important" and the other "Least Important"
- Bulletins from last week's service or copies of order from worship leader
- Song lyrics, hymnals, and prayers associated with service
- Visual focus and sound maker*
- Slips of paper with a reading from the daily lectionary for the coming week (see *Reflection and Prayer*, p. 104)
- Music player, quiet instrumental music

Tasks

- *Discussion*
    - —*Choosing Scripture for worship*: Speak with a pastor or worship planner to become familiar with how Scripture is chosen for worship and how Scripture is incorporated into different elements of worship in your community.
    - —Cut up the solutions to the word search, so one text can be given to each youth.
    - —Write the three methods for choosing Scripture on chart paper or a chalkboard.
- *Reflection and prayer*
    - —Ask your pastor to recommend daily lectionary readings that are used in your congregation.
- Consider inviting a pastor or worship planner to join the group for this module.

---

*   See page 6 in the introduction for the suggested use of a distinctive sound and visual focus or worship centre for your *Reflection and prayer* time.

Session

Opening activity: Word search (10 minutes)

The word search introduces the diversity found within the Bible and the reality that not all texts are of equal importance. Divide the youth into pairs. Provide each pair with a copy of the word search (handout), a pencil or pen, and a Bible.

Instruct youth to search for words and match them to the passages, OR look up passages to identify the words hidden in the word search.

Solutions:

Genesis 1:27	*humankind, female*
Genesis 27:11	*hairy*
Matthew 22:36-40	*commandment, prophets*
Exodus 23:19	*boil*
John 3:16	*believes*
Matthew 6:9-10	*Father, kingdom*
1 Samuel 24:2	*three, relieve*
Psalm 23:1-3	*shepherd, restores*
Genesis 36:20	*Horite, Oholibamah*
Psalm 139:1-3	*searched*
Luke 6:27-28	*enemies, bless*
Psalm 137:9	*dash*
Matthew 5:14-16	*light, works*
Job 39:5	*wild*
Deuteronomy 6:4	*Israel*
Leviticus 11:20-21	*detestable, jointed*
Romans 16:14-15	*Asyncritus, Olympas.*
1 Corinthians 13:4-5	*patient, arrogant*

Discussion: Choosing Scripture for worship (15 minutes)

Teaching moment: The Bible is the starting point for planning worship. While it is important to include lots of Scripture in worship, not every verse in the Bible is an equally valid foundation for a worship service. We have to choose which parts of Scripture to use in our worship.

Group line-up discussion

This is a subjective exercise that should prompt discussion.

- Place the two sheets of paper with "Most Important" and "Least Important" at opposite ends of the room.
- Assign one of the texts from the opening activity to each youth.
- Ask the youth to position themselves in the room according to how important they think their text is for congregational worship.
- When they are finished, ask them to explain their reasons for picking that spot.

Teaching moment: There are different ways of choosing Scripture for worship. Explain the lectionary, theme, and book study approaches described in Content for Teaching and Learning. *Give an example of each, if possible, from your own congregation's worship. Point out that it is possible to combine various methods.*

Small group discussion

Divide into three groups. If your class has more than 12 students, make more than three groups. Assign each group one of the methods (lectionary, theme, book study). Groups should answer the following questions:

1. What are the strengths of this method?
2. What are the weaknesses of this method?
3. What patterns, themes, or books would you want to use to plan worship?

Large group discussion

Bring the group back together and invite each small group to share their answers to the questions.

Discussion: Incorporating Scripture into every part of worship (15 minutes)

Teaching moment: The Bible is incorporated into every part of worship, not only during Scripture reading. Sometimes Scripture is read or spoken directly, as with the Lord's Prayer. At other times it inspires the words of a worship leader or song writer, such as Matt Redman, whose "Blessed be your name" is inspired by Job 1:20-22.

Small group discussion

Divide into small groups of 3 to 5 youth. Give each group a copy of a bulletin or written description of worship and the resources necessary to interpret it. Suggest they first read the primary Scripture text of the service. Ask them to then write on the bulletin or description where this passage and other parts of the Bible have been incorporated into the service and how they have been included.

Large group discussion

Invite the small groups to share their results to the following questions:

1. Where is the Bible incorporated into the service?
2. How has it been incorporated?

Ask the group to think of other places and ways the Scripture could be incorporated.

Reflection and prayer: Reading Scripture devotionally (5 minutes)

Gather around the visual focus.

Teaching moment: We can pick Scripture for our personal Bible study or prayer time using the same three methods.

1. *We can follow a lectionary or schedule of readings.*
2. *We can read through whole books of the Bible.*
3. *We can look for passages associated with a particular theme.*

We will be talking about how to use Scripture in worship during our class time for the next two weeks. We can also read Scripture together even when we're apart. We can be connected to each other through our Scripture reading. We can become a "scriptural community."

Give each person a Bible and slip of paper with a lectionary reading from the week. Ask the youth to read the passage and think about it. Use the distinctive sound to start the quiet time, and play quiet music as the youth reflect. Make the sound again to bring the group back together. Close with prayer.

Example for closing prayer:

> *Living God, we thank you for the words you have given us in the Bible. We expect these words to change our lives and our world. Help us to find ways to use your words in the worship of our community and our daily lives so that your Word can direct us as a lamp for our feet and a light for our path. Amen.*

Bible Word Search

See reverse for clues.

```
C Q D H S A D K G B B S E A R C H E D T N X H Y
O H A M A B I L O H O H U I S H A I R Y N N P X
M A R R O G A N T H R E E B R I Z R E H T A F H
M Y D P A F X O E L A M E F D E T N I O J L U R
A L E A R S I D E T E S T A B L E P U C R M G X
N N K N R E L I E V E R P H O R I T E K A F P S
D V N P R O P H E T S B Y S U T I R C N Y S A A
M D L I W I D D R E H P E H S W O R K S G T E E
E M O D G N I K E N E M I E S P P I X K H Q H L
N X L I O B S E R O T S E R Z A N P A G O N I B
T B X T O O L Y M P U S X A T D Q P I I N T V Z
A R N I W L P A T I E N T H G B E L I E V E S N
```

Bible Word Search

Genesis 1:27 God created _____ in his image, in the image of God he created them; male and _____ he created them.

Genesis 27:11 Jacob said to his mother Rebekah: "Look, my brother Esau is a _____ man."

Matthew 22:36-40 "Teacher, which _____ in the law is the greatest?" Jesus said to him, " 'You shall love the Lord your God with all your heart, and with all your soul, and with all your mind.' This is the greatest and first commandment. And the second is like it: 'You shall love your neighbour as yourself.' On these two commandments hang all the law and the _____."

Exodus 23:19 You shall not _____ a kid in its mother's milk.

John 3:16 For God so loved the world that he gave his only Son, so that everyone who _____in him may not perish but may have eternal life.

Matthew 6:9-10 Pray then in this way: Our _____ in heaven, hallowed be your name. Your _____ come. Your will be done, on earth as it is in heaven.

1 Samuel 24:2 Saul took _____ thousand chosen men out of Israel, and went to look for David and his men in the direction of the Rocks of the Wild Goats. He came to the sheepfolds beside the road, where there was a cave; and Saul went to _____ himself.

Psalm 23:1-3 The Lord is my _____, I shall not want. He makes me lie down in green pastures; he leads me beside still waters; he _____ my soul.

Genesis 36:20 These are the sons of Seir the _____, the inhabitants of the land: Lotan, Shobal, Zibeon, Anah, Dishon, Ezer, and Dishan; these are the clans of the Horites, the sons of Seir in the land of Edom. The sons of Lotan were Hori and Heman; and Lotan's sister was Timna. These are the sons of Shobal: Alvan, Manahath, Ebal, Shepho, and Onam. These are the sons of Zibeon: Aiah and Anah; he is the Anah who found the springs in the wilderness, as he pastured the donkeys of his father Zibeon. These are the children of Anah: Dishon and _____ daughter of Anah.

Psalm 139:1-3 O Lord, you have _____ me and known me. You know when I sit down and when I rise up; you discern my thoughts from far away. You search out my _____ and my lying down, and are acquainted with all my ways.

Luke 6:27-28 Love your _____, do good to those who hate you, _____ those who curse you, pray for those who abuse you.

Psalm 137:9 Happy shall they be who take your little ones and _____ them against the rock!

Matthew 5:14-16 You are the _____ of the world. A city built on a hill that cannot be hid. No one after lighting a lamp puts it under a bushel basket, be on the lampstand, and it gives light to all in the house. In the same way, let your light shine before others, so that they may see your good _____ and give glory to your Father in heaven.

Job 39:5 Who has let the _____ ass go free?

Deuteronomy 6:4 Hear, O _____: The Lord is our God, the Lord alone.

Leviticus 11:20-21 All winged insects that walk upon all fours are _____ to you. But among the winged insects that walk on all fours you may eat those that have _____ legs above their feet, with which to leap on the ground.

Romans 16:14-15 Greet _____, Phlegon, Hermes, Patrobas, Hermas, and the brothers and sisters who are with them. Greet Philologus, Julia, Nereus and his sister, and _____, and all the saints who are with them.

1 Corinthians 13:4-5 Love is _____; love is kind; love is not envious or boastful or _____ or rude.

Reading and Listening to Scripture in Worship

Module focus

How can we read Scripture so that the congregation can hear God's message? How can we listen to Scripture expecting to hear God's message? This module explores techniques for reading and listening to Scripture in public worship. Following this module, consider inviting more confident Scripture readers to prepare for and read Scripture in upcoming church services.

Leader preparation

Materials

- Copies of *Handouts 1* and *2* (p. 110 and p. 111) for each pair of youth
- Printed Scripture texts, a different text for each participant
- Bibles
- Pens/pencils
- Visual focus and sound maker*

Tasks

- *Discussion and preparation for worship*
  —Familiarize yourself with the background information on reading Scripture.
  —Choose and print Scripture texts from an online Bible source, double-spaced and in 14-point type. Try to select familiar texts or sections recently studied in Sunday school or used in worship. Select a range of texts for the diverse abilities of the group: easier, short narrative passages and longer, more difficult poetic texts. Avoid extremely difficult texts.
  —Pick an item (names, God's actions, human emotions or instructions on how to live) from each text for which you want the group to listen.
  —Reserve the worship space for your meeting time.
  —If your congregation has a sound system operator, ask that person to join the group.
- *Reflection and prayer*
  —Identify the Scripture passage the youth will be preparing to present in worship in Module 3 (p. 112).

---

* See page 6 in the introduction for the suggested use of a distinctive sound and visual focus or worship centre for your *Reflection and prayer* time.

Session

Opening activity: Tongue Twister Face-off (8 minutes)

Test out some tongue twisters listed on *Handout 1* by repeating the phrases at increasing speeds. Starting with number 1, have individuals face off in pairs to see who can read the same phrase the most times quickly without slipping up. The winner of each pair progresses to the next round. Continue until the two top tongues vie for victory using the most vicious verse.

If members of your group speak English as a second language, invite them to share tongue twisters in their native languages. If there are youth who struggle with speech invite them to help judge the competition.

Option

Play the party board game Mad Gab® in which one player sounds out puzzles while others guess the phrase formed by the words. For example, when pronounced quickly "These If Hill Wore" sounds like "The Civil War." Bible Mad Gab® using phrases from the NIV translation of the Bible is also available.

Discussion and preparation for worship (25 minutes)

Teaching moment: Reading Scripture should be the high point of a worship service. It is not an introduction to the sermon, but a time when we hear God's Word to us. Unfortunately, reading Scripture often does not receive careful attention. Today we are going to practice reading Scripture for each other.

Individual preparation (9 minutes)

Give each person a printed passage, a copy of *Handout 2: Reading Scripture*, a Bible, and pen or pencil. Ask the youth to prepare a Scripture reading, following the instructions on the sheet. Since time is limited have them pay particular attention to points 1, 4, 5, 6, 7, and 8.

Practicing in pairs (5 minutes)

Divide youth into pairs. Have one person read the passage out loud while the partner listens. All readers can read aloud simultaneously. When the readers are finished, they may ask their partners these questions:
  —Who was the reading about?
  —What was the central action or idea?
Reverse roles and repeat the exercise.

Practicing together (10 minutes)

Move the group to the worship space. If possible, use the sound system. Ask them to volunteer to read their passages one at a time, standing where the person reading Scripture usually stands.

Ask the rest of the group to line up at the back of the worship space and listen for the item you chose for that reading. Each time they hear what they are listening for, they take a step forward. When a new person begins reading, have the group move back to the wall.

At the end of the exercise, encourage the youth to keep the handout as a reference for future times when they read Scripture.

Reflection and prayer: *Lectio Divina* (12 minutes)

Gather the group around the visual focus.

Teaching moment: Lectio Divina *is Latin for "divine reading." It is an ancient spiritual discipline that invites us to listen to the word of God and make it relevant for our lives. Today we are going to read and reflect on the passage we will present to the congregation.*

Practicing Lectio Divina

NOTE: If the group will be presenting a longer portion of Scripture, choose a short excerpt for this exercise.

- Begin with the distinct sound.
- Give the italicized instruction and then read the text clearly and slowly.
- Pause after each reading for 10 seconds of silence before inviting discussion.
  1. First reading. *During the first reading just take in the passage. Don't analyze; just get the general sense of what it is about.* Read. Pause.
  2. Second reading. *Listen for one word or phrase in the passage that "shimmers" or reverberates with you, a word that attracts or disturbs you. Be prepared to share your word or phrase with the group.* Read. Pause. Share quickly in a circle.
  3. Third reading. *Think about how the word that struck you connects with your life right now. How does it relate to what you have seen and head today? How does it relate to home, school, friends, community, family, fun, or the world? Invite another leader to read.* Pause. Share reflections.
  4. Fourth reading. *How is God present in the connection between Scripture and life? How is God calling you and others to respond?* Read. Pause. Share reflections.

What questions arise from this passage for you? A pastor will be preaching on this text in a few weeks. What questions and issues would you suggest the sermon address?

- Lead the group in a short prayer. For example: *Living God, you speak to us and the situations we face every day through the ancient words of the Bible. (Prayers of thanks and intercession for the issues raised during the time of reflection). Amen.*
- End with the distinctive sound.

Tongue-Twister Challenge

1. A box of biscuits, a batch of mixed biscuits.
2. A noisy noise annoys an oyster.
3. A skunk sat on a stump and thunk the stump stunk, but the stump thunk the skunk stunk.
4. Can you imagine an imaginary menagerie manager imagining managing an imaginary menagerie?
5. Crisp crusts crackle crunchily.
6. Fat frogs flying past fast.
7. Flash message!
8. Fred fed Ted bread, and Ted fed Fred bread.
9. Gertie's great-grandma grew aghast at Gertie's grammar.
10. Give papa a cup of proper coffee in a copper coffee cup.
11. Greek grapes.
12. How much wood would a woodchuck chuck if a woodchuck could chuck wood? He would chuck, he would, as much as he could, and chuck as much wood as a woodchuck would if a woodchuck could chuck wood.
13. I thought a thought. But the thought I thought wasn't the thought I thought I thought.
14. If one doctor doctors another doctor, does the doctor who doctors the doctor doctor the doctor the way the doctor he is doctoring doctors? Or does he doctor the doctor the way the doctor who doctors doctors?
15. If Stu chews shoes, should Stu choose the shoes he chews?
16. Inchworms itching.
17. Lesser leather never weathered wetter weather better.
18. Many an anemone sees an enemy anemone.
19. Of all the felt I ever felt, I never felt a piece of felt which felt as fine as that felt felt, when first I felt that felt hat's felt.
20. Old oily Ollie oils old oily autos.
21. Say this sharply, say this sweetly, Say this shortly, say this softly. Say this sixteen times in succession.
22. Selfish shellfish.
23. Six short slow shepherds.
24. Six sick slick slim sycamore saplings.
25. Sixish.
26. Swan swam over the sea, Swim, swan, swim! Swan swam back again Well swum, swan!
27. The two-twenty-two train tore through the tunnel.
28. Twelve twins twirled twelve twigs.
29. Unique New York.
30. We surely shall see the sun shine soon.
31. Which witch wished which wicked wish?
32. Which wristwatches are Swiss wristwatches?
33. You've no need to light a nightlight On a light night like tonight, For a nightlight's light's a slight light, And tonight's a night that's light. When a night's light, like tonight's light, It is really not quite right To light nightlights with their slight lights on a light night like tonight.

Reading Scripture

Preparing to read

1. Read the text and make sure you understand its meaning.
2. Choose what translation of the Bible you will use. Check to see if a specific version is used in your congregation.
3. Consider printing a copy of the text in larger print, with double spacing..
4. Mark pauses and words you wish to emphasize.
5. Plan how you will introduce the text. For example, "A reading from the gospel according to Matthew, Chapter 5."
6. Use proper names for people who were introduced earlier in the chapter or book. You can also give a short description, or set the scene. For example: Paul sent this message to the Corinthian church. In this passage, he is talking to the leaders of the church.
7. Plan how to conclude the text. For example, certain congregations conclude Scripture readings with a phrase such as, "This is the Word of the Lord. Thanks be to God!"
8. Read through the text several times aloud before the worship service.
9. Record yourself at least once, so you can hear how you sound.
10. Read the passage for others and ask them for feedback.

When you read Scripture . . .

- *Speed.* Read slowly. Add pauses in appropriate places.
- *Tone.* Clearly begin and end each sentence. Avoid raising your voice in a "question" at the end of a sentence, or allowing it to drop off at the end of a phrase.
- *Form.* The Bible includes history, story, prophecy, poetry, song, teaching, and law, among other forms of material. Read in a manner appropriate to the form of the text. For example, tell a story, rather than simply reading it.
- *Content.* The Bible reflects many different thoughts and emotions. Read a passage in a way that reflects its content. For example, read a description of the crucifixion sorrowfully, and an account of the resurrection joyfully.
- *Posture, gestures, and eye contact.* Stand still and keep your hands still. Consider placing your hands on the lectern. Memorize how you will introduce the reading and look at the congregation as you make the introduction. Feel free to look at the text rather than the congregation while you read. Memorize the final phrase of the passage and look up again at the end.
- *Listen.* Listen to yourself reading the Scripture text. Focus on the message, not on your technique or the audience.
- *Engage.* Be responsive to what the passage is saying to you. Let the text come to life in you. Let the text bring you to life. Let it show!

Creatively Presenting Scripture in Worship

Module focus

How can we bring the Bible to life for the congregation? This module prepares the group to present a Scripture text or several texts dramatically during the Sunday service.

Leader preparation

Materials

- Random objects in boxes, baskets, or bags (colander, hockey stick, scarf, light bulb, sunglasses, laundry basket, etc.)
- Copy of chosen Scripture drama for each participant (see *Tasks, Preparation For Worship*)
- Costumes and/or props
- Visual focus and sound maker*

Tasks

- *Preparation for worship*
    - —Communicate with worship planners and leaders about your contribution to the service.
    - —Find a dramatic version of the Scripture for the service in one of the *Resources* (p. 100) or online. Do not be afraid to adapt the drama so it is suitable for your group and context. Consider using a second, simpler reader's theatre if you have a larger group, or if other participants may wish to be involved at the last minute.
    - —Prepare necessary costumes or props.
    - —Think through the staging of the drama and make notes for yourself. Remain open to the ideas and suggestions of the youth, but do not expect to make every staging decision by consensus.
- Invite a member of the congregation with drama experience to assist the group.
- Expect to spend additional time preparing the drama.

---

* See page 6 in the introduction for the suggested use of a distinctive sound and visual focus or worship centre for your *Reflection and prayer* time.

Session

Opening activity: Random objects drama game (15 minutes)

Divide the group into several small groups of 3 to 7 people. Give each group a box, basket, or bag with 7 random objects (including the container). Allow 5 minutes for groups to prepare a familiar Bible story that incorporates all of the objects and every member of the group. Present the dramas.

Preparation for worship: Drama rehearsal (28 minutes)

Explain the drama and when it will be shared with the congregation. Assign parts and read through the script once. Try acting it out, preferably in the worship space. You can make changes as you rehearse.

Make sure you take into account the sound system and the layout of the worship space, so all actors can be seen and heard. A list of useful tips for presenting Scripture-based dramas is included in *Word of Mouth* by Craig Morton and Ken Hawkley (see resource list, page 100).

People who won't be there when the drama is shared can prepare costumes and props, make pictures or sets, or act as understudies when others have to miss rehearsal. They can also be "the audience" and provide feedback about the show.

It will likely take more than one session to adequately prepare the drama. Consider spending additional sessions on rehearsal or finding an alternative time to prepare.

Reflection and prayer (2 minutes)

Gather around the visual focus. Begin with the distinctive sound. Dedicate the work of the group to God with a short prayer. For example:

Active God, you tell your story with vivid words and images in Scripture. Be with us as we invite our community into your story, so that we can be a part of your continuing story in the world. Amen.

End with the distinctive sound.

Youth Worship Leadership Suggestions

Scripture drama

- Work with an accessible text. Narrative portions of Scripture are usually the simplest to portray dramatically and the easiest for youth to understand.
- Choose or write a script that reflects the size and character of the group. Do not be afraid to adapt existing material.
- Place the Scripture drama at an appropriate point in the service. Especially if humour is involved, consider how it will enhance or disrupt the flow of worship.
- Consider inviting the children to come forward so they have a better view.

Getting creative

- Instead of acting out the drama in worship, make a movie. This works well if you have plenty of time before the Sunday you are leading worship. You could use a youth retreat to prepare and shoot the movie. Make sure you allow time for editing as well as filming.
- Tell a story or express an idea using still photos of members of your group.
- Invite someone who knows American Sign Language to teach the group how to sign the text.
- If the words of Scripture are projected in worship, design backgrounds and illustrations that illuminate the meaning of the passage.
- Create a visual that builds as the passage develops.
- Read the scriptural text or parts of it in different languages. This can be particularly meaningful at Pentecost or when Scripture speaks of "all nations" praising God.
- Consider writing your own script if a small group of youth express interest and are able make an additional time commitment. Advice on writing Scripture drama is included in the book *Word of Mouth*.
- Include recorded music or congregational song in your dramatic presentation.
- Invite audience participation in the drama.
- Have one person read the text while others act it out.
- Find ways to use the whole worship space, if sound equipment permits.
- Frame Scripture reading with song, gesture or posture to highlight its importance.

Youth worship leadership checklist: Scripture

Spiritual

1. Do the youth have an opportunity to pray together before the service?
2. Have youth been given adequate opportunity to reflect on the meaning of the text for their own lives, the community, and the world?
3. Is the presentation of the drama true to the meaning of Scripture?
4. Do the youth have the opportunity to celebrate and evaluate the service several days later?

Logistical

1. Are all scripts, props, and costumes present?
2. Are all youth and leaders aware of when they will be involved in the service and how and when they will move to and from their seats to where they will be leading worship?
3. Is the sound system prepared, and have youth been instructed on how to use the microphones so each word can be heard by the congregation?
4. Are others involved in leading the service, including the worship leader, preacher, and sound operator, fully aware of how and when the youth will be involved?

Preaching

Unit focus

In many congregations, preaching is the core of the worship service. The sermon is often the longest single element in a worship service. The sermon should give us an opportunity to listen to and apply God's word. A good preacher will challenge us to live out what we have heard.

Unit 7 teaches youth about the nature and purpose of preaching and how to listen and respond to a sermon. The unit prepares youth to preach a sermon collaboratively. Be ready to add additional modules for sermon preparation. Module 3 begins the process but does not provide enough time for the sermon to be refined.

It is possible for each module in Unit 7 to stand alone. It would be valuable to pair this unit with a Bible study on the text preached by the youth, or to choose a text that has been the subject of a recent Bible study. Unit 1, Module 2 (p. 17) could also be added to this unit for additional instruction on public speaking.

Unit outline

Content for Learning and Teaching
    Introduction to preaching
    Listening to preaching
    Types of sermons
    Sermon structure
    Good preaching
    Writing for the ear
    Alternatives to listening
    Resources

Curriculum Modules
    Module 1: Introduction to Preaching
    Module 2: Listening and Responding to Preaching
    Module 3: Preaching Together

Youth Worship Leadership Suggestions
    Getting creative
    Youth worship leadership checklist

Content for Learning and Teaching

Introduction to preaching

A sermon is the intersection of a word from God and human need that results in new life through the presence of the Holy Spirit. During the rest of the service, we address our words to God, but during the sermon, we hear God's word.

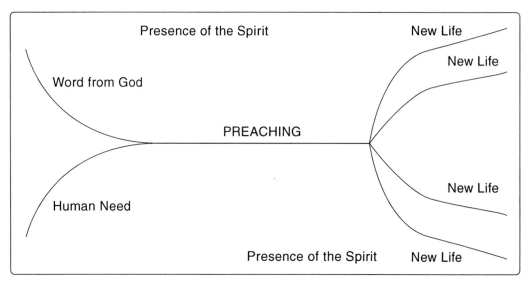

This definition and diagram are borrowed from *Preparing Sunday Dinner* (see resources, page 119).

Listening to preaching

Learning to listen to a sermon is the first step toward transformation. Here are a few helpful hints:

1. *Expect transformation.* Expect to hear God speaking to you through the words of the preacher. Expect to be convicted. Expect to accept God's grace. Approach the sermon with a positive attitude.
2. *Stay alert* with your body as well as your mind. Maintain good posture. Avoid slouching or dozing off. Get adequate sleep the previous night.
3. *Use active listening.* Think of the sermon as a conversation. Note your reactions (both intellectual and emotional) to the material presented.
4. *Identify the sermon structure.* Recognizing the structure of a sermon allows you to follow the message of the sermon and track the preacher's progress.
5. *Take notes.* Note-taking promotes active listening, clarifies structure, and allows for further reflection in the future.
6. *Respond to the message.* Respond to the sermon immediately, as invited during worship. Change your daily life in response to the message.
7. *Reflect later.* Remember the message or review your notes in the weeks following the service.
8. *Discuss your ideas with others.* Engage other members of the congregation or friends and family in discussing the message.
9. *Focus on one idea, phrase, or word that catches your attention.* Do not worry about understanding or remembering every part of the sermon.

Types of sermons

Preaching can be divided into two primary categories:

- Preaching that argues a point
- Preaching that tells a story

Many preachers combine these approaches.

Sermon structure

Sermons can be organized in different ways. Different sermon structures are appropriate for different subject matter. Common structures include:

1. *Sermons containing one point:* address one clear idea from several angles
2. *Sermons containing multiple points:* lay out several clear ideas in a direct, propositional way, possibly concluding with an application
3. *Verse-by-verse:* interprets each verse of a scriptural text in turn
4. *Thesis-antithesis-synthesis:* presents one aspect of God or Scripture, explores the limitations of this interpretation, and brings the two perspectives together to form a mediating or alternative position
5. *Journey to celebration:* moves through blocks of material, ending with celebration of what God has done or is doing, intended to empower the community
6. *Theological quadrilateral:* addresses a theme from the perspective of Scripture (how the Bible speaks to the topic), tradition (how the church has addressed the theme in the past), reason (theological perspectives on the subject), and experience (application to contemporary life)
7. *Narrative:* tells a story that identifies a problem, evaluates the issues, hints at resolution, presents the good news in light of the problem, and anticipates the consequences
8. *Persuasion organization:* intends to bring about change—gets the attention of listeners, identifies a need, presents a solution, explores how the solution addresses the need by visualizing the results, clarifies the action that must be taken by listeners to achieve the results

Good preaching

The Eastern Mennonite Seminary Preaching Institute states that the following characteristics define good preaching:

- Expository (grounded in the biblical text)
- Relevant (speaking to contemporary hearers)
- Inspiriting (engendering hope through judgment and grace)
- Prophetic (delivering a word from the Lord)
- Communal (co-creating with listeners the meaning of God's message)
- Evangelical (proclaiming God's good news)
- Charismatic (empowered and directed by the Holy Spirit)
- Invitational (calling people to follow Jesus in the world)
- Captivating (holding people's attention)

Writing for the ear

Writing a sermon is not like writing an essay. The congregation does not read the message, but hears it; the sermon must be written for the ear rather than the eye. Use common sense; preach a sermon you would want to listen to. Here are a few helpful tips to keep in mind:

1. Show—don't tell—your listeners. Use vivid, visual language. Illustrate from life. Engage the senses. Use concrete examples, rather than abstract ideas.
2. Write the way you would speak.
3. Make sure your audience, intention, and words match. Use language that connects with the context.
4. Be yourself. Do not try to imitate someone else's preaching style.
5. Don't ask permission or apologize.
6. Get to the point. Remove unnecessary information and assumptions.
7. Tell stories.
8. Use simple language whenever possible.
9. Use fresh and vibrant language.
10. Ask questions (Do we . . . ?) rather than conjecture (I wonder . . .).

Alternatives to listening

A particular topic, preacher, or life circumstance might make it difficult to listen to preaching at times. Instead of using the time during the sermon to plan your social schedule or worry about the upcoming week, consider using the time to:

- Pray.
  —Think over the events of the past week and anticipate events in the coming week in the world, your community, and your life. Pray about them.
  —Pray for the people surrounding you in the church or in the community.
- Read the Bible.
  —Read the text that is the basis of the sermon, and then read the sections of Scripture before and after.
  —Read through a book of the Bible during the sermon.
- Read the hymnal.
  —If there are hymnals in the pews, read through hymn texts and reflect on the words. Start with the hymns for the service and then explore other sections.
- Reflect on the sermon topic.
  —Think of stories from your own life related to the sermon topic.
  —Ask yourself: What would you preach about if you were addressing the topic? Do you have questions about the topic?

Be careful not to prevent those around you from listening to the sermon. Remember, alternatives to listening are secondary to learning to listen well.

Resources

Preaching

Greiser, David B. and Michael A. King, ed. *Anabaptist Preaching: A Conversation Between Pulpit, Pew and Bible.* Telford, PA: Cascadia Publishing House, 2003.

Jacks, G. Robert. *Just Say the Word! Writing for the Ear.* Grand Rapids: William D. Eerdmans, 1996.

Yoder, June Alliman, Marlene Kropf and Rebecca Slough. *Preparing Sunday Dinner: A Collaborative Approach to Worship and Preaching.* Scottdale, PA: Herald Press, 2005.

Listening to preaching

The Mennonite Handbook. Scottdale, PA: Herald Press, 2007.

Introduction to Preaching

Module focus

Why is preaching important? What are different types of sermons? What makes a sermon good or bad? This module explores the purpose and nature of preaching.

Leader preparation

Materials

- Tennis balls
- Chalkboard and chalk *or* chart paper and markers
- Paper
- Pens/pencils
- Visual focus and sound maker*
- Bibles
- Music player
- Musical version of Luke 1:46-55 (Mary's song)

Tasks

- *Opening activity*
  —Choose Tennis Debate topics.
- *Discussion*
  —Familiarize yourself with *Content for Learning and Teaching* (p. 116).
- *Reflection and prayer*
  —Find a musical version of Mary's song, the Magnificat (Luke 1:46-55), to play during the reflection (for example: "My Soul Is Filled with Joy"—*Sing the Journey CD 1*; "My Soul Cries Out"—*Sing the Story CD 1*.)

* See page 6 in the introduction for the suggested use of a distinctive sound and visual focus or worship centre for your *Reflection and prayer* time.

Session

Opening activity: Storytelling game (10 minutes)

Go around the circle creating a simple story, with each person adding one word.

Option

If the group is more creative, consider adding a phrase or sentence per person. With more than 18 youth, form two groups.

Opening activity: Tennis debate (10 minutes)

Divide into teams of about four people, and have teams face each other in parallel lines. Provide each pair of teams with a tennis ball.

The teams will debate funny subjects with two clear sides. *Examples*: Who would win in a fight, a caveman or an astronaut? The Lion King is better than Star Wars. Would Jesus use a Mac or PC? Assign one line to represent each side.

The teams must toss the tennis ball back and forth every 15 seconds, making points and responding to each other's arguments. Have a different team start the debate for each topic.

Option

Apples to Apples®, a party game also involving argument, is another option. Read the instructions that accompany the game. Encourage youth to argue for different cards, not necessarily their own.

Teaching moment: Preachers try to do different things in sermons. Two common preaching patterns are: 1) telling a story, and 2) arguing a point. There are also different ways to organize the content of a sermon. Different structures are appropriate for different subjects. Common structures include . . . (Introduce the structures included in the Content for Learning and Teaching *and write them on the board or chart paper.)*

Discussion (15 minutes)

Remembering past sermons (5 minutes)

Large group discussion

Ask the group if anyone can remember something about a sermon they have heard. If necessary, ask follow-up questions:

- Does anyone remember a sermon that used a prop or visual image?
- Does anyone remember the topic of a sermon or who preached it?
- Does anyone remember a story from a sermon you found interesting or moving?
- Does anyone remember a sermon that used one of those structures (for example, Martin Luther King Jr. often employed the "Journey to Celebration" structure)?

Qualities of good sermons (5 minutes)

Teaching moment: Sometimes we are hesitant to identify certain sermons as good or bad or better or worse, because we care about our preachers and know they are doing their best. Also, different people appreciate different types of sermons, so it is difficult to identify better or worse sermons. At the same time, it is clear that certain sermons are better or worse than others.

Small group discussion

Divide the youth into small groups of 3 to 5. Invite each group to think back on sermons they remember, in their home congregation or in other contexts.

- Ask each group to identify what made these sermons good.
- Ask each group to list at least five qualities of good sermons.

Large group discussion
After several minutes, gather as a large group and collect the ideas of the small groups. Introduce the *Qualities of Good Preaching* found in *Content for Learning and Teaching* (p. 116) and compare the list to that of the youth.

Purpose of preaching (5 minutes)
Small group discussion
Return to the small groups and ask them to come up with an answer to this question: What is the purpose of preaching?

Large group discussion
After all groups have determined an answer, gather as a large group and invite the small groups to share their responses. Are the responses the same? Do they address different aspects of preaching?

Teaching moment: A sermon should take a passage from Scripture, present possible interpretations of the passage, and give ideas about ways to apply the Scripture to our everyday lives. It should also challenge us to make changes in our relationship with God, each other, and all creation.

To illustrate this idea, draw on the board or chart paper the diagram included in the *Content for Learning and Teaching.*

Reflection and prayer (10 minutes)
Gather around the visual focus. Introduce the prayer exercise.

Teaching moment: In prayer, human need intersects with God's word. Today we will pray for the needs in our community and world that emerge when we reflect on a passage of Scripture. We will read Mary's Song (Luke 1:46-55) and each think of one need in our community or world related to this text. After a time of reflection, we will pray for these concerns in short sentences: for example, "We pray for the homeless."

Give each youth a Bible, paper, and a pen or pencil. Begin a time of quiet reflection with the distinctive sound, and play softly a musical version of Mary's Song.

Refocus attention with the sound, and begin the prayer, giving time for the youth to offer their concerns emerging from the text. For example:
Living God,
You continue to speak to the needs of our community and our world through Scripture.
(Youth speak sentence prayers.)
You hear all of our prayers, spoken and unspoken.
Amen

Listening and Responding to Preaching

Module focus

How can we listen and respond to preaching? This module explores how youth can develop the skills of listening and responding to preaching.

Leader preparation

Materials

- Chalkboard and chalk *or* chart paper and markers
- Paper
- Pens/pencils
- Visual focus* with lighted candle
- Small candle for each participant
- Matches
- Sound maker*

Tasks

- *Opening Activity*
  —Prepare four or more lists of 20 words (see examples in activity).
- *Discussion*
  —Familiarize yourself with the *Listening to Preaching* and *Alternatives to Listening* in *Content for Learning and Teaching* (p. 116).

---

* See page 6 in the introduction for the suggested use of a distinctive sound and visual focus or worship centre for your *Reflection and prayer* time.

Session

Opening activity: Word Memory (15 minutes)

- Divide the youth into teams of four to six, and then divide each team into two even groups.
- Provide each group with a printed list of 20 words (see examples below—each list should be different).
- Give each group 2 minutes to think of ways to present their words to the other half of their team, so they will remember all of them (acting out the words, telling a story, making an acrostic poem or drawings, saying them in different tones of voice, making letters with their bodies, etc.). Every member of the group must be involved in presenting the words.
- The group has 3 minutes to present as many words as possible. The words may not be written down by either part of the team.
- Groups then take turns presenting their lists to the other halves of their teams. Invite one team to present their lists at a time.
- After each list is presented, the other group has 1 minute to remember as many of the words as they can. Add together the number of words remembered by both groups on each team. The team that remembered the most words wins.

Sample word list:

Penguin	Beautiful	Hurry	Hot
Hospital	Skateboard	Hotdog	Scurry
Photo	Preach	Autumn	Purple
Run	Is	Grow	Jesus
Tango	Summer	Gigantic	Skiing

Option 1

With a small group, have one person present the list and the entire group remember the words.

Option 2

To illustrate the teaching moment below, tell one team they must only read the list, but allow the other team to be creative in their presentations.

Option 3

Use an alternative memory game that encourages listening carefully.

Discussion: Listening to sermons (18 minutes)

Teaching moment: It was much easier to listen to and remember lists of words when the groups presented them in interesting and creative ways. It would have been harder to remember if I had stood here and read the list in a dull monotone. Preaching is often the same way.

Divide the youth into small groups of 3 to 5. Give each group three sheets of paper and pens. One at a time, read the teaching moments in Parts 1, 2, and 3, and present the corresponding tasks. Give the groups two minutes to discuss and complete their lists, and then invite them to share their responses with the whole group. Consider writing the responses on the board or chart paper.

Part 1—Learning to listen

Teaching moment: Today we will think more about how we can learn to listen and respond to sermons. What we "get out" of preaching is closely related to what we "put in." Preaching is one opportunity to hear what God is saying to us in our lives today. It is an opportunity to be changed so we can become more like Jesus.

Task 1

> List 5 ways to "put more in" to listening to preaching.

> After each group has shared their response, present the *Listening to Preaching* list from *Content for Learning and Teaching* (p. 116).

Part 2—Preaching topics

Teaching moment: Sometimes it can be hard to listen and pay attention to sermons, especially when preachers choose stories, words, and examples that don't relate to us.

Task 2

> List 5 topics or parts of the Bible you would want to hear a sermon about.

> After each group shares their list, pass the topics on to the pastor or preaching team

Part 3—Alternatives to listening

Teaching moment: Sometimes the sermon topic or your life circumstances make it hard to listen. For instance, you might not relate to a sermon on end of life choices.

Task 3

> List 5 things you can do during a sermon, other than listening, that keep you focused on God, the Scripture, and how it applies to your life.

> After each group has shared, present the *Alternatives to Listening* list from *Content for Learning and Teaching*.

Reflection and prayer: Listening to each other (12 minutes)

Gather around a visual focus that includes a lighted candle. Instruct each person to remember the high point and low point of the person who shares after they do (the last person remembers what the first person shared). They should choose two words, one associated with the high and the other the low, to remember.

- Go around the circle, inviting each person to share a high point and low point from the past week. Pause a moment between persons to facilitate remembering what was shared.
- Distribute small candles, one to each person.
- Begin a time of prayer with the distinctive sound.
- Go around the circle again. Have each person light the candle and place it near the visual focus while saying the two words they chose for the person who shared after they did.
- Open and close the prayer with words such as:
  > *Listening God, You hear all our prayers. We offer to you what we have heard from each other . . . You hear all our prayers, spoken and unspoken. Amen.*
- End the prayer with the distinctive sound.

Preaching Together

Module focus

How can we preach a sermon together? Module 3 presents a model for preaching a sermon together as a youth group. The first steps for preaching together are included in the module. Expect to spend two to four additional sessions preparing and rehearsing the sermon.

Leader preparation

Materials

- 50 objects (basketball, paper clip, wooden spoon, crayon, shampoo, apple, sunglasses, light bulb, maracas, perfume, etc.)
- Opaque bag
- Chart paper and markers
- Copy of the handout (p. 130) for each small group
- Bibles and simple Bible commentaries
- Paper
- Pens/pencils
- Visual focus and sound maker*

Tasks

- *Opening activity*
  - —Gather objects and place them in a large, opaque bag.
- *Preparing for worship*
  - —Review the *Content for Learning and Teaching* on preaching in this unit (p. 116), *Writing Words for Worship* in Unit 4 (p. 72), and *Speaking Words in Worship* in Unit 1 (p. 17).
- Familiarize yourself with the *Model for Preaching Together* (p. 127) and adapt it for your group and congregational context.
- *Before the session*:
  - —Pray for the youth and congregation and the process of preparing to preach. Listen to how the Spirit is leading the group to contribute to worship.
  - —Communicate clearly with others involved in leading the service in which the youth will be preaching. Speak with a regular preacher about how he/she is involved in planning other aspects of the service. Expect to fill these coordination roles.
  - —Choose a Scripture text to serve as the basis for the sermon. Ideally, this should be a text the group has worked with recently in Bible study or Sunday school. It is generally easier to work with narrative texts. Abstract theological or poetic material is more challenging.
- Invite a pastor or preacher to join the group for this module.

---

* See page 6 in the introduction for the suggested use of a distinctive sound and visual focus or worship centre for your *Reflection and prayer* time.

Session

Opening activity: Mystery Object (10 minutes)

This game gets the group thinking about using vivid language that shows rather than tells.

- Divide the youth into two teams.
- Instruct each team to send one member behind a screen or door.
- Have a leader hand one object at a time from the bag to the team member behind the door.
- Give the team member 30 seconds to get the rest of the team to guess as many objects as possible by describing the objects, using only the five senses—sight, touch, taste, smell, and sound. (The person cannot describe what the object does, what it is used for, or when it is used. The purpose is to *show* the group the object, using words, rather than *tell* the group about the object. For example, to describe a basketball, the speaker can say it is orange, spherical, about one foot in diameter, and feels like it is covered in small raised bumps. He/she cannot say it is used to play a team sport, or that it is dribbled and shot through a hoop.)
- One point is awarded for each correctly guessed object, and one point is taken away each time the rules are broken. The team with the most points at the end wins.

Preparation for worship: Preaching together (32 minutes)

Explain that the group will preach a sermon together. Introduce the Scripture text that will be the starting point for the sermon. Identify the core message of the text using the different models explained in Option 1 and Option 2 below. Option 1 calls on you to do the ground work ahead of time. Option 2 requires a group study process, and for this you may want to plan an extra session to study the text. Both options break down a single sermon that can be prepared and preached by small groups or individual youth.

Model for preaching together
Option 1

In this option, the youth identify one simple sentence associated with their point. They then expand on the sentence, creating a sermon that both expounds on their theme and applies it to everyday life. The handout and module focus on Option 1.

- Study the text yourself. Extract approximately five key points (either phrases or actions) from the passage. Each phrase or action should have enough scope for a small group to prepare a 3- to 5-minute message. For example, using the parable of the sower (Luke 8:4-15), five key points might be: 1) The sower goes to sow; 2) The seed on the path is trampled; 3) The seed on the rock withers; 4) The seed among the thorns is choked; and 5) The seed on good soil produces an abundance.
- Write the five key phrases on chart paper to serve as a reference for the group.
- Write the Scripture text and a different phrase on each copy of the handout "Preparing to Preach Together."

Option 2

This option results in four or five groups of youth expanding on the central message from different perspectives. This option requires additional research on the part of the youth and more communication between groups.

- Consider adding an additional module to this unit that is a Bible study of the chosen text.
- Youth will extract a key message (one simple sentence) from the text that addresses a congregation need.
- There are two possible methods for writing the sermon:
    —Theological quadrilateral: 1) Scripture, 2) history, 3) theology, 4) experience, and 5) application
    —Problem-solution, or law-gospel approach in which four groups address: 1) problem in Scripture, 2) problem in our lives, 3) solution in Scripture, and 4) solution in our lives.
- Copy the handout (p. 130) and write the Scripture text and one perspective on each copy.
- Involve some or all of the youth in the preparatory work.

Small group discussion

Form small groups of two or three youth to work on different parts of the sermon, as described above. Give each group a copy of the handout, paper, pens or pencils, a Bible, a Bible commentary, and other helpful resources. Instruct them to work through the handout using their phrases.

Pray before the groups begin to work. For example:

Living God, be present in us as we prepare to share your word with our community. May your Spirit guide our thoughts and conversations. Amen.

Be prepared to assist the groups as they work through the handout. By the end of the module, expect each group to have determined a message and purpose for their portion of the sermon, as well as a list of ideas to incorporate.

Large group discussion

Invite each small group to share their message and purpose statements with the large group. See how the messages and purposes fit together and if any adaptation is required. Ensure that each group is only communicating one key idea.

Continuing writing

Expect to spend several more modules refining and rehearsing the sermon. Review the *Content for Learning and Teaching* on *Writing for the Ear* in Unit 7 (p. 118), *Writing Words for Worship* in Unit 4 (p. 72), and *Public Speaking Tips* in Unit 1 (p. 10) with the group.

Connecting the sections

Consider linking the potentially disjointed parts of the sermon together with a visual image. For the story of the sower, for example, you might plant a seed, add images of path, rock, and rich soil to a banner, or project an image at the beginning or end of each section of the sermon. Consider singing the same short song between sections, or using the same sentence to begin each part of the sermon. Consider choosing a song to precede or follow the sermon.

Option

Have pairs or small groups who are not comfortable preaching work on other aspects of worship that surround the sermon (for example, the Scripture reading, time with children, song of response, and sermon visuals—either projected or physical).

Prayer (3 minutes)

Gather around the visual focus. Beginning and ending with the distinctive sound, pray for God's continuing guidance in the process of preparing to preach together. For example:

God, you have given us an exciting opportunity to speak your word to our community. We recognize this is also a big responsibility. Guide our thoughts and words and we prepare to preach together. Amen.

Preparing to Preach Together

Bible Text: _____

Key Phrase: _____

1. Read the entire Scripture text twice, aloud.

    Who is it about? _____

    What is happening? _____

    Where does your phrase fit into the story? _____

2. Reflect on what the phrase in the text means to you.

    With which character do you identify? _____

    Does this happen in your life? _____

    What questions does it raise for you? _____

3. Read about the text in a Bible commentary.

    How does the commentary add to your understanding of the phrase?
    _____
    _____

4. Reflect on what the text means for the congregation.

    How does it relate to specific recent events in lives of individuals, the community, and the world?
    _____
    _____

    How does it encourage the community?
    _____
    _____

    How does it challenge the community?
    _____
    _____

    How does it call the community to change?
    _____
    _____

5. Decide on a sermon message—a simple, one-sentence statement that summarizes the one thing you want to say to the congregation. For example, a sermon message may be, "God's love sustains us in difficult times," or "Faith requires strong roots to survive."

6. Write a sermon purpose, naming what you hope to accomplish. For example, a sermon purpose could be to "Remind the congregation of God's sustaining love," or to "Celebrate God's sustaining love in the congregation."

7. Brainstorm ideas, experiences, stories, and songs relating to the message and purpose of the sermon, or the phrase or text.

Youth Worship Leadership Suggestions

Integrating youth into preaching

- If only one or two members of your group are comfortable preaching, invite them to prepare sermonettes while the rest of the group prepares a presentation for the children, Scripture reading, and song of response.
- If two or more youth are preaching independently, consider inviting them to choose their own texts from a common theme, perhaps one from the Old Testament and the other from the New Testament. They could also preach on the same text with different focuses (for example, an individual focus and a communal or global focus).
- If a youth has a positive experience preaching a shorter sermon, invite him or her to preach a full-length sermon during the summer or at another convenient time.
- Make sure youth know adult leaders are there to support them throughout the process. At the same time, make sure the youth are preaching their own sermon, not adult leaders' sermons.

Getting creative

- Instead of preaching a traditional sermon, have each group design a sensory centre in a different location in the sanctuary, based on a phrase. Consider including a Scripture text, questions for reflection, and some form of response (for example, planting a seed or writing a prayer). Engage all of the senses. Invite the congregation to wander around to the different centres while music plays. Ensure you have enough centres for the size of the congregation.
- Consider how God's word can be proclaimed in drama, dance, and art during the sermon.
- Prepare a sermon directed especially at children, with relevance for the rest of the congregation. Invite the children to the front and use all of the senses to engage their attention and the attention of the congregation.

Youth worship leadership checklist: Preaching

Spiritual

1. Do the youth have the opportunity to pray together before the service?
2. Does the sermon address the needs of the congregation?
3. Is the sermon true to Scripture?
4. Do youth feel comfortable and confident with the message and purposes of the sermon?
5. Do the youth have the opportunity to celebrate and evaluate the service several days later?

Logistical

1. Have other individuals planning and leading the service been fully informed as to how and when the youth will be involved in preaching?
2. Is it clear who is speaking or reading each part of each segment of the sermon?
3. Is it clear how the preachers will move from where they are seated to where they are preaching, and back?
4. Are transitions between sermon segments, including visual and musical elements, prepared and rehearsed?
5. Are visual elements and musical elements ready?
6. Is all technical equipment fully operational, and are all preachers familiar with how to use sound equipment?

The Body and the Senses

Module focus

Worship is physical as well as intellectual and emotional. It engages all our senses: sight, sound, touch, taste, and smell. Although silence and meditation may be one element of worship, worship is not an inward retreat from the world, but an active engagement with our surroundings.

Unit 8 explores the physical and multisensory dimensions of worship. The youth will contribute to worship through adapting existing worship elements and resources to engage all of the senses.

The two modules may be used individually; however, Module 1 is a useful brainstorming exercise for Module 2. Additional sessions for planning and rehearsal may be required. These modules can also be combined with Unit 2, Module 3 (p. 37) or Unit 4, Module 3 (p. 76), to write multisensory opening and closing words or a prayer that engages all of the senses.

Unit outline

Content for Learning and Teaching
> Traditional ways of involving the body and the senses
> Expanding traditional ways to use the senses in worship
> Resources

Curriculum Modules
> Module 1: Movement in Worship
> Module 2: Planning Multisensory Worship Together

Youth Worship Leadership Suggestions
> Leading multisensory worship
> Getting creative
> Youth worship leadership checklist

Content for Learning and Teaching

In this unit, especially in Curriculum Module 2, we draw on content from other units (listed under "tasks"), since they already touch on aspects of the body and the senses in worship. Here, we simply take a panoramic view the many ways all worship involves our bodies and senses, and we imagine ways to engage our bodies and senses in even more diverse ways.

Traditional ways of involving the body and senses in worship

Hearing. In the worship traditions that most Mennonites know, there is great emphasis on speaking and listening, which involve our tongues, voices, and our ears. The spoken, sung and heard word has been central.

Sight. The simplicity of many Mennonite worship spaces reflects values of simplicity and humility. The written word is often read in printed materials including Bibles, hymnals and bulletins. Physical gestures and movements have an obvious visual element. Posture, eye contact and dress are all part of the visual presentation of worship. Historically, Mennonites have not emphasized visual art in church, although that is changing.

Physical gestures, touch, and movements. We often are not conscious of how these can help or hinder worship. Good speakers use effective hand gestures and avoid excessive or distracting movement in the pulpit. The symbolic actions we take in baptism, Communion, and foot washing also involve the body—whether kneeling for baptism, eating at Communion, or rubbing warm water on a partner's feet during foot washing.

Taste and smell. Mennonites historically have not consciously promoted the use of these senses; we do not use incense, for example, to symbolize our prayers rising to God. However, taste is part of our Communion experience.

Expanding traditional ways to use the body and senses in worship

Mennonites today are open to engaging the body and the senses in new ways. The following are some ways that are becoming increasingly common, suggesting that we want to present our whole beings to God:

Hearing. Beyond new forms of music, some churches use bells or other instruments to call people to prayer or signal an element in worship.

Sight. Art, candles, worship displays, and banners—these have often been acceptable during Christmas or other high seasons. More and more, their symbolism is becoming important as a regular feature of worship. Similarly, the symbolism of the colours of the Christian calendar is increasingly recognized as a way of strengthening our appreciation of the gospel message of the seasons. Objects placed on the communion table are being discovered as powerful way to focus worship, especially for people who rely on the visual for learning and worship. Projecting images, words, diagrams, photographs, video clips and more is part of weekly worship in many churches.

Physical gestures, movement and touch. Liturgical dance is sometimes used to express the emotion of a Scripture passage, song, or prayer that is offered in worship. Gestures such as passing the peace with handshakes or hugs, clapping, actions that accompany singing, and processing forward with the offering or to receive communion are also being practiced more frequently. Anointing with oil during a healing ceremony or smudging our foreheads with ashes at the beginning of Lent are becoming more common expressions of our commitments and our longings during worship.

As we look to the future, Mennonite churches can think about even more diverse and creative ways to engage all of the sense in our worship of God. For suggestions see the "Getting Creative" section at the end of the unit as a starting point. Consider how you can invite individuals in your community to share their gifts.

Resources

Kimball, Dan. *Emerging Worship: Creating Worship Gatherings for New Generations.* Grand Rapids: Zondervan, 2004.

Yoder, June Alliman, Marlene Kropf and Rebecca Slough. *Preparing Sunday Dinner: A Collaborative Approach to Worship and Preaching.* Scottdale, PA: Herald Press, 2005.

Krahn, Karmen and Leslie James. *Proclamation by Design: The Visual Arts in Worship.* Scottdale, PA: Faith & Life Resources, 2008.

Physical Movement in Worship

Module focus

How do we worship God with our bodies in corporate worship and daily life? This module explores how worship is physical and the physical activities of our lives are worship.

Leader preparation

Materials

- Chart paper and markers
- Play dough (large piece for each team)
- 12-inch lengths of yarn in 8 colours (brown, green, purple, orange, pink, yellow, blue, red), enough so each person has one of each
- Small zip-close bags
- Visual focus and sound maker*

Tasks

- *Opening activity*
    —Prepare a list of words and phrases relating to how we use our bodies in daily life (see examples, p. 135). Set up a partition.
- *Discussion*
    —Prepare a list of words and phrases relating to how we use our bodies in worship. (see example, p. 136)
- *Reflection and prayer*
    —Prepare a small bag for each person with different coloured yarn.

* See page 6 in the introduction for the suggested use of a distinctive sound and visual focus or worship centre for your *Reflection and prayer* time.

Session

Opening activity: Simultaneous Speed Charades (10 minutes)

This game serves as an opening activity and begins the discussion portion of the module.

- Divide the group into two teams.
- Separate the teams with a wall or partition, so they cannot see each other.
- Have each team send one team member to a leader to receive the word or phrase.
- The chosen team member must get their team to guess the word or phrase using physical motions and no words, sounds, letters, or symbols.
- The team that guesses the word first wins.
- If neither team can guess after 1 minute, move on to the next person and word or phrase.

Words and phrases should reflect ways we use our bodies in everyday life:

sleeping in	fighting	playing capture the flag
eating breakfast	talking with your hands	hula hooping
sports at school	carrying a heavy object	breathing
gymnastics	driving a car	singing in a choir
hugging	swimming	
reading and writing	basketball tournament	

Option

With a small group, have one person act out a word or phrase while the rest of the group guesses.

Discussion: Worshipping God with our bodies every day (8 minutes)

Teaching moment: We can worship God with our bodies through all of these actions and many more in everyday life. For example, through playing on the school basketball team, we stay healthy, make friends, and work together.

Small group discussion

Divide each team into small groups of 3 to 5 youth. Give each group chart paper and markers. Have them list answers to the question: How can we use our bodies to worship God in our everyday lives?

Large group discussion

Gather as a large group. Invite each small group to share their list. Ask them to expand on how several specific actions listed can be a form of worship. For example, how can brushing your teeth worship God?

Game: Simultaneous Speed Sculpterades (10 minutes)

Using the same two teams and partition or wall division as in Speed Charades, play Simultaneous Speed Sculpterades to begin the discussion of how we use our bodies during Sunday morning worship.

- Give each team a large piece of play dough.
- Each team sends one member to a leader to receive the word or phrase.
- The chosen team members must get their teams to guess the word or phrase by sculpting the play dough without using words, sounds, letters, symbols, or actions. For example, "hug" must be conveyed, not by hugging another person, but by shaping two play dough people who hug each other.
- The team that guesses the word first wins.
- If neither team can guess after 1 minute, move on to the next sculptor and word or phrase.

Words and phrases should reflect ways we use our bodies in corporate worship:

singing	drinking communion juice	walking to church
sitting and standing	placing offering in the plate	folding hands
passing the peace (shaking hands)	clapping	opening and closing eyes
smiling and laughing	walking in and out of the church	raising hands
speaking and listening	playing instruments	dancing
kneeling	holding a hymnal	watching the leader
eating communion bread	biking to church	

Option

With a small group, have one person sculpt a word or phrase while the rest of the group guesses.

Discussion: Worshipping God with our bodies in Sunday worship (8 minutes)

Teaching moment: Through all of these actions, and many more, we can worship God with our bodies when we gather for worship at church.

Small group discussion

Divide each team into small groups of 3 to 5 youth. Give each group chart paper and markers. Have them list answers to the question: How can we use our bodies during worship? Encourage creativity. Don't worry about what is or is not realistic.

Large group discussion

Gather as a large group and invite each small group to share their list. Ask them to expand on how several specific actions listed can be a form of worship. For example, how can wearing clothes, dancing, or stretching be ways to worship God?

Reflection and prayer: Thanking God for caring for our bodies (9 minutes)

Gather around the visual focus. Give each person a bag with different colours of yarn. Explain the time of reflection and prayer: "As we take each colour of yarn, we will thank God for a different way God provides for and cares for our bodies. Use the yarn to make a tassel, a long string, a braid, etc."

Encourage each person to find some personal space in the room. Begin and end the prayer with the distinctive sound. Pause after each sentence.

Prayer:

Creator God, we thank you for the many ways you nourish us and care for us, including our bodies.

*As we take the **brown** yarn, we say thank you for your mysterious role as Creator of life and at the beginning of each of our lives. You knew us and cared for us even before we were born . . .*

*As we take the **green** yarn, we say thank you for the food we eat—the energy it provides for our bodies and the delicious flavours we enjoy. We pray for those who do not have enough to eat . . .*

*As we take the **purple** yarn, we say thank you for our health, for medical professionals who care for our bodies, and scientific researchers who find new ways of healing. We pray for those who suffer from poor health . . .*

*As we take the **orange** yarn, we say thank you for sports, for opportunities to stay healthy, have fun, and make friends . . .*

*As we take the **pink** yarn, we say thank you for the beauty of our bodies, in all of their different shapes and sizes. We pray for those who have difficulty recognizing themselves as your beautiful creation . . .*

*As we take the **yellow** yarn, we say thank you for family, including our church family, who care for our physical needs. We pray for those who struggle to provide for their families or who struggle with broken family relationships . . .*

*As we take the **blue** yarn, we say thank you for friends, including our friends here today. We thank you for handshakes, hugs, and the other ways we show how much we care about each other . . .*

*As we take the **red** yarn, we say thank you for Jesus, through whom you became human and experienced our physical reality. You embrace the world of sight, sound, touch, taste, and smell with us . . .*

Thank you God, for the bodies we live in. Help us to use them to worship you and serve others, through the power of your Spirit living in us. Amen.

Planning Multisensory Worship Together

Module focus

How can we engage all of our senses (sight, sound, touch, taste, and smell) in worship? This module invites the youth to adapt worship elements and resources to engage all the senses.

Leader Preparation

Materials

- Copy of the handout (*Worship Mad Libs*, p. 141) for each pair of youth
- Pens/pencils
- Order of worship for planned service
- List of ideas from discussion in Module 1 (p. 135), 1 copy for each small group
- Paper
- Bibles
- Resources chosen for service
- Sources for additional worship resources
- Visual focus and sound marker*

Tasks

- *Opening activity*
  —Make copies of the handout and cut them in half. *Or* prepare a sensory opening activity based on the specific Scripture text and theme for the service to which the youth will contribute.
- *Discussion*:
  —Determine elements of worship youth can plan and lead in conjunction with the worship planner for the service (see *Preparation for Worship*, p. 139).
  —Select enough elements so that small groups can work on different aspects of the service.
  —Consider selecting worship resources in advance that the youth can adapt to become multisensory.
  —Bring an order of worship for the service and be prepared to explain the biblical story, theme, and structure.
  —Review the *Content for Learning and Teaching* on *Choosing words for worship* (p. 26) and *Resources* for finding worship resources (p. 27) in Unit 2.
- *Reflection and prayer*
  —Become familiar with the practice of breath prayer.
- Invite the worship planner of the service to which the youth are contributing to be present for the module.

---

* See page 6 in the introduction for the suggested use of a distinctive sound and visual focus or worship centre for your *Reflection and prayer* time.

Session

Opening activity: Worship Mad Libs (10 minutes)

This activity gets the group thinking about different physical movements that might be used in worship. Divide the group into pairs.

- Give each pair a copy of the right-hand side of the Mad Lib handout (list of required words). Allow 5 minutes to fill in the words.
- Distribute the left-hand side (description of worship service). Instruct them to fill in the blanks.
- Invite pairs to read their Mad Libs aloud to the group.

Option

Use a sensory illustration for the central text or theme of the service to which the youth will contribute. How you do this depends on the story or theme itself. For example:

- Eat the food described in the story.
- Have a paper boat-folding contest, if the text relates to water.
- Look at pictures of physical ailments, if it is a story of healing.
- Play cymbals and tambourines.
- Bring in objects relating to the story, or contemporary parallels that convey the same ideas.
- Take a few minutes to write cards or letters to friends far away, if the reading is from an epistle.

Choose an activity that connects the story or theme to your immediate sensory experience. Conclude by reading the text and explaining the theme of the service.

Preparation for worship: Planning multisensory worship together (30 minutes)

Divide into small groups of 2 to 5 to plan different elements of the service. For example, small groups could work on:

- Beginning of worship
- End of worship
- Confession and reconciliation
- Offering prayer
- Congregational prayer
- A particular song
- A ritual to respond to the sermon

With a very small group, consider preparing one element together.

Teaching moment: Explain the elements the group will contribute to worship that you have chosen in conjunction with the worship planner. Emphasize that the goal is to think about the physical aspects of different parts of the service, and how you can incorporate your bodies and all of your senses into these elements. If you used the Worship Mad Libs for the opening activity, briefly introduce the text and theme of the service.

Small group discussion: Multisensory worship elements

Give each small group paper, pens or pencils, and the list of ideas for physical movement in worship collected in Module 1. Groups will spend several minutes listing ways that all of the senses could be engaged in the particular element of the service they are preparing. Remind them to write everything down. Invite each small group to report back to the large group.

Small group discussion: Multisensory worship texts and themes

Give each small group a Bible, any worship resources related to the service (for example, opening words, prayers of confession, etc., from a series) or collections of worship resources. Consider choosing resources for each part of the service in advance and inviting youth to adapt them so they are multisensory.

Alternatively, youth can choose or write worship resources themselves that relate to the text or theme of the service, and make them multisensory. Each small group can use the approach of their choice.

Invite each small group to reflect on their element of the service from the perspective of the theme or text and record their ideas. How can multisensory dimensions relating to the theme or text be incorporated into their part of the service? Look to the preceding discussion for inspiration.

Large group discussion

Gather the groups back together and report ideas. See how the ideas fit together and adapt as necessary to engage different senses in different parts of the service,

Small group discussion: Attention to detail

Give each small group time to refine their ideas and prepare to present them to the congregation. Additional sessions may be required to prepare for the service, depending on the worship elements designed by the youth. Ensure that they pass on any specific instructions, or need for supplies or equipment.

Reflection and prayer: Breath prayer (5 minutes)

Gather around the visual focus.

Teaching moment: The "breath prayer" or "Jesus Prayer" is an ancient prayer practice that uses breathing to guide the prayer. We pray with the whole body, not just the mind. When we pray this prayer, we say one phrase as we inhale and another phrase as we exhale.

Encourage each person to find a personal space in the room. Begin with the distinctive sound and give the following instructions as the youth pray:

Sit still, in a comfortable position, and take deep, slow, quiet breaths in and out.
(Pause.)
As you inhale, breathe God's spirit into your body. As you exhale, picture your worries and thoughts floating away from you.
(Pause, breathing in and out slowly, 4 or 5 times.)
With each inhale, silently pray the words: "Lord Jesus Christ."
(Pause.)
With each exhale, silently pray the words: "Have mercy on me."
(Speak an example aloud. "Lord Jesus Christ, have mercy on me.")
Continue breathing and praying for several minutes.

Explain that many other simple phrases from Scripture can be used as breath prayers, for example: "The Lord is my shepherd . . . I shall not want" (Psalm 23), "I come to you . . . give me rest (Matthew 11:28), and "Be still . . . and know that I am God (Psalm 46:10).

Ask the youth to use the breath prayer during the week. End with the distinctive sound.

Worship Mad Libs

Day of the week _____

Time _____

Physical Location 1 _____

Name of a Person 1 _____

Verb 1 _____

Noun 1 - Living Thing _____

Name of a Person 2 _____

Noun 2 - Household object _____

Religious Concept 1 _____

Movie Character _____

Verb(ed) 2 _____

Name of a Song 1 _____

Action using feet _____

Name of a Person 3 _____

Location within physical location 1 _____

Adjective 1 - physical quality _____

Adjective 2 - emotional quality _____

Noun 3 - unusual object _____

Location 3 - unusual location _____

Verb 3 - something done to something else _____

Adjective 3 _____

Noun 4 - any object _____

Verb(ed) 4 _____

Religious Concept 2 _____

Verb(ed) 5 - action of a group _____

Name of a Person 4 _____

Food 1 _____

Treasured Possession _____

Drink 1 _____

Liquid _____

Verb(ed) 6 - any action using neither feet nor hands _____

Verb(ed) 7 - group action _____

Verb(ed) - any action _____

Name of a Song 2 _____

Name of a Dance _____

Verb(ed) 9 _____

Length of Time _____

Name of a Person 5 _____

Abstract Quality _____

One (day of the week _____) around (time _____) a group of people gathered at (location 1 _____) for a worship service. It began when (name 1 _____) went to the front of the sanctuary and started to (verb 1 _____). Soon everyone joined in and began to (verb 1 _____) as well. Next thing you know the (noun 1 _____) arrived. (Name 2 _____) soon put a stop to it all by waving a (noun 2 _____) in the air. "This (noun 2 _____) symbolizes (religious concept 1 _____)" they said. "And it is just like when (character _____)(verb 2 _____). Let us respond by singing (song 1 _____) and (action _____)."

Then (Name 3 _____) stood (location within location 1 _____) and (adjective 2 _____). "Let us pray: O God, you are (adjective 1 _____). You are like a (noun 3 _____) in the (location 3 _____). You (verb 3 _____) us always but in ways we do not understand. You are (adjective _____). Amen."

Then each person took a (noun 4 _____) and (verb 4 _____) it as a symbol of (religious concept 2 _____).

Next all (verb 5 _____) to prepare for the ritual. Then (name 4 _____) took (food 1 _____) and said, "On the night he was betrayed Jesus took (food 1 _____) and broke it saying; this is my (possession _____) broken for you." (Name 4 _____) then took (drink 1 _____) and said "And then he took (drink 1 _____) poured out for many." And said this is my (liquid _____) and drank the (drink 1 _____). And all ate the (food 1 _____).

All (verb 7 _____) and (verb 8 _____). All sang (song 2 _____) and danced a (dance _____). And when it was over they (verb 9 _____).

And afer (length of time _____), (name 5 _____) said, "Go in (abstract quality _____)."

Youth Worship Leadership Suggestions

Leading Multisensory Worship

- Use the gifts of the youth. They naturally engage the world in a multisensory fashion. Encourage them to use this ability in worship planning and leadership.
- Be attentive to context. Using new ways to worship God may make the congregation uncomfortable at first. Be aware of possible conflicts or discomfort.
- Keep it simple. Sensory worship does not need to be complicated. It can be as simple as encouraging people to shake hands with each other at the beginning of the service or hold hands during a prayer. It can mean creating a visual display, or providing rhythm instruments, as appropriate, during songs.
- Don't overload the senses. Incorporate sensory elements throughout the service on a regular basis, but avoid making worship too complex and difficult to follow.
- Involve children, but do not limit sensory worship to children. Children connect especially well with sensory aspects of worship, but it is also valuable for youth and adults.
- Consider creating centres in the worship space, as an alternative or addition to a sermon, to address the story or theme from a different sensory perspective.
- Find multisensory worship ideas in the Getting Creative sections throughout the *Sourcebook*.

Getting creative

Sight

- While the offering is collected, project images of members of the congregation doing the work of God during the week.
- Adjust the lighting in the worship space during different parts of the service (for example, dim the lights during a time of quiet prayer).
- Add to a visual display throughout the service.
- Provide paper and pencils for sketching responses to the sermon.
- Illustrate the sermon with art or movie clips.

Sound

- Begin worship with a sound relating to the theme of the service, such as an alarm clock, siren, cymbal, or rainstick.
- Have a time of silence, when you ask people to listen for sounds inside and outside the building. Ask them to pray for joys and concerns related to the sounds (cars—people on trips; baby crying—new parents; coughing—people who are sick, etc.)
- Illustrate the sermon with sound (for example, a violent conflict or joyful celebration).

Smell

- Although incense has been traditionally associated with high church traditions, it can be used in any worship service if an appropriate explanation is provided. Explain the symbolism of incense and the way it was used in the tabernacle.
- Pass items connected with the theme of the service to make a story or text more immediate (for example, freshly baked bread, flowers, or honey).
- Be aware of any severe allergies in the congregation related to scents, flowers, etc.

Taste
- The Lord's Supper is an occasion where taste is an important part of worship. Consider emphasizing this during a communion service.
- Add taste elements to illuminate other stories, such as the feeding of the 5,000 or the Passover.

Touch
- Plant seeds or bulbs the congregation can watch grow in the coming weeks.
- Distribute stones and invite each person to come forward and place a stone at a certain place.
- Distribute play dough or modeling clay to aid reflection on a theme or as a form of response to the sermon. For example, shape bowls during a confession, to represent emptying ourselves to be filled by God.
- Invite the congregation to come forward and light candles.
- Embrace the sensory elements within the Mennonite tradition: foot washing, the Lord's Supper, and passing the peace.

Youth worship leadership checklist: The body and the senses

Spiritual
1. Do the youth have the opportunity to pray together before the service?
2. Has an appropriate context for multisensory worship been created (for example, explaining verbally and noting in writing that youth are leading elements of worship with particular attention to engaging all of the senses)?
3. Do the youth have the opportunity to celebrate and evaluate the service several days later?

Logistical
1. Are clear instructions provided for the congregation regarding how and when they can participate and the meaning of their participation?
2. Are all necessary supplies in position?
3. Is required technical equipment fully operational?
4. Are youth aware of where they need to be, what they are doing, when they are doing it, and what it means?

Offering

Unit focus

Receiving the offering is a meaningful moment of personal commitment and an intersection between daily life and Sunday worship. This unit addresses stewardship in the context of the church budget, personal giving, and the time during which the offering is received in worship.

The youth will lead the offering through a combination of: the invitation and prayer of dedication, offertory music, a visual or dramatic presentation of the church budget, and receiving the offering as ushers. If your congregation does not receive the offering during the service, consider encouraging reflection on other forms of giving with a creative presentation, prayer, or song at an appropriate point.

Modules 1 and 2 can be used independently. Consider using Module 1 (on the church budget), prior to a congregational meeting that will discuss the budget, replacing the time of reflection with the opening activity from Module 4. This will help youth better understand the proceedings or the resulting conversations at home. Module 2 (on personal giving) may be particularly appropriate at the beginning of a new academic, fiscal, or calendar year.

Unit outline

Content for Teaching and Learning
 Offering as worship
 Offering in worship
 Budget language
 Resources

Curriculum Modules
 Module 1: The Budget
 Module 2: Personal Giving
 Module 3: Offering as Worship
 Module 4: Leading the Offering Together

Youth Worship Leadership Suggestions
 Leading the offering
 Getting creative
 Youth worship leadership checklist

Content for Teaching and Learning

Offering as worship

- Offering is an act of worship. We give as an expression of faith. Giving is a spiritual practice that enables us to grow in faith and love.
- We give to God. We do not give to buildings, budgets, or the church, although God's work may be done through these things.
- Giving to God is a priority. We give our first and best to God, not our leftovers.
- Giving is both our responsibility and a delight. Everyone has something to give, and the more we give, the more we want to give.
- Our focus is where our money is, therefore, we should give to things we care about, but also things we want to care about.

Offering in worship

There are many ways to receive the offering in the context of a worship service. Three actions often shape the offering portion of the worship service:

- *Invitation*: a brief introduction to the offering (two or three sentences)
  - —Identifies our giving as a grateful response to God's gifts
  - —Connects our giving to the theme or Scripture of the service
  - —Explains how our offerings serve God
  - —Explains the process of the offering reception
- *Reception*: giving and receiving the offering
  - —Congregation gives the offering, which is either brought forward by members of the congregation, given by direct bank deposit, or gathered by the ushers
  - —Additional offerings, such as food or volunteer commitment forms may be received
  - —Music often accompanies the reception of the offering
- *Dedication*: presenting the offering to God and devoting it to God's purposes
  - —Spoken prayer of thanksgiving and dedication. For example: "Generous God, you gave us life; now we give our lives back to you" (David J. Randolph, *HWB* 751)
  - —Hymn or song of dedication. For example: "Take my life, and let it be" (Frances R. Havergal, *HWB* 389)

These actions may take place in any order, and two or more of them may be combined.

Budget language

Budget: Plan created at the beginning of the fiscal year, estimating how much money will be received and deciding how money will be spent.

Surplus: Funds left over at the end of the fiscal year, after all bills have been paid

Deficit: Amount still owed at the end of the fiscal year.

Debt: Accumulation of deficits over multiple years

Mortgage: Specific loan taken out to purchase property or building, usually repaid over a period of 10–30 years. If the interest on the loan is not repaid as agreed to, the lender takes over the building or land. Mortgages are used to purchase a building or add an addition.

Pre-authorized remittances (PAR, other terms): Offering given by means of automatic bank withdrawals

Resources

Youth Stewardship Curriculum

Vincent, Mark and Michele Hershberger. *Moneytalk: Living Generously: Bible-based Explorations of Issues Facing Youth.* Generation Why Bible Studies vol. 6:2. Scottdale, PA: Faith & Life Resources, 2000.

Stewardship Resources

Friesen, Edwin. *First Things First: A Study Guide.* Winnipeg: Mennonite Foundation of Canada, 2007.

Miller, Lynn A. *Firstfruits Living: Giving God Our Best.* Second Edition. Scottdale, PA: Herald Press, 2004.

Moyer Suderman, Bryan. *My Money Talks: Songs for Worship.* smallTall Music, 2007 http://www.smalltallmusic.com/

Vincent, Mark. *A Christian View of Money: Celebrating God's Generosity.* Scottdale, PA: Herald Press, 1997.

Vincent, Mark. *Money Mania: Mastering the Allure of Excess.* Living Stewardship Series. Goshen, IN: MMA Stewardship Solutions, 2005.

The Budget

Module focus

Where does the church's money come from? How is the money spent? What difficult budget decisions must be made? This module provides a basic introduction to the church budget, through a game in which two teams face off at various budget-related events.

Leader preparation

Materials

- Music player and music
- Copy of church budget
- Scoreboard (see *Discussion—The Church Budget Game*, p. 149)
- Timer
- Chart paper and markers
- Visual focus and sound maker*
- Prayerful music on theme of budgeting time

Tasks

- *Opening activity*
  - —Choose a theme for the game that mirrors an event in popular culture: for example, the playoffs in a popular sports league or a recent movie.
  - —Select music relating to the theme—for example, a movie theme song, team song, or sports warm-up music (Classic pump-up songs include "Get ready for this" by 2 Unlimited, and "We will rock you" by Queen, but use music that is appropriate in your context.)
- *Discussion*
  - —Talk to those in charge of finances in your church (church treasurer, stewardship and finance committee, or pastor). Ask for a copy and explanation of the church budget, statistics relating to congregational giving, and an overview of any current financial issues.
  - —Set up a scoreboard.
  - —Develop about 25 true/false questions based on giving statistics, basic budget terminology (see *Budget language*, p. 145), and financial structures for your congregation. For example:
    1. The budget is the amount of money spent by the church over the course of the year. (*False*)
    2. Total giving has, on average, been increasing over the past 10 years.
    3. The budget is the plan created at the beginning of the fiscal year, estimating how much money will be received and spent. (*True*)
    4. The year with the highest giving in the past 10 years was_____ .
    5. A debt is the difference between the money you spend and the money you get in a single year. (*False*)
    6. A deficit is the difference between the money you spend and the money you get in a single year. (*True*)

---

* See page 6 in the introduction for the suggested use of a distinctive sound and visual focus or worship centre for your *Reflection and prayer* time.

7. The church has had a deficit for the past 10 years.

8. A debt is the accumulation of deficits. (*True*)

9. The members of the congregation who are over 65 give only a tiny portion of the budget.

10. The members of the congregation who are between 25 and 45 give ___ per cent of the budget.

11. The members of the congregation between 45 and 65 give the highest amount of money per person.

12. More than ___ people contribute to our church budget.

—For "Showcase Showdown," develop colourful descriptions of five "showcases" (as in the game show "The Price is Right"), based on how significant portions of your church budget are used—total budget (be sure to include this one), Christian education, property management, staff, etc. For example:

Property Management! Property management includes keeping our church building standing, heated, lighted, and clean. It keeps water flowing through the toilets and computers humming in the office. Property management ploughs the snow in the winter and cuts the grass in the summer. What is the value of this Showcase? Place your bids now! Actual value: $74,400.00

—Choose a topic related to the current financial situation of your congregation to debate.

• *Reflection and prayer*

—Choose prayerful music related to giving. Suggestions: "Take my life, and let it be"—Frances R. Havergal (*HWB* 389); "Better is one day in your house"—Matt Redman; "Seasons of Love"—Rent; "Jesus be the centre"—Michael Frye, 1999 (*STS* 31)

• Invite the church treasurer or another leader involved in stewardship and finance to join the group for this module.

Session

Opening activity: Pre-game warm-up (4 minutes)

As youth arrive, play music relating to the theme you have chosen (movie, sports playoffs, etc.). Divide the group into two equal teams. If you have more than 10 youth per team, consider creating more teams. If you have five youth or less, form a single team. Ask each team to choose a team name and prepare to play the Church Budget Game.

The Church Budget Game (36 minutes)

Two teams compete in three events that track the church budget, from beginning to end. The team that wins the most events wins the game. Keep track of progress on the scoreboard.

Where does the church's money come from? (10 minutes)

Define a region that is the "safe," using a broom closet, tables turned on end, or a square marked with tape on the floor. All of the youth should be able to fit into the "safe," but it should be a tight squeeze. If there are four teams, create two "safes."

- Teams take turns answering the true or false questions you prepared, about your church budget.
- Each time a team answers correctly, a team member goes in the "safe." If a question is answered incorrectly, a team member must leave the "safe." *Note: People in the "safe" can no longer answer questions, but questions may be repeated, so all participants should listen closely throughout the game.*
- The first team to put all their team members in the "safe" wins.

Showcase showdown: How is the money spent? (10 minutes)

Give each team chart paper and markers to write down their bids. Begin with the Showcase based on the total budget, to give youth a sense of the size of your church budget.

- Read a Showcase description and give one team 25 seconds to write down their bid for the value of the Showcase.
- Give the second team 15 seconds to make their bid. (If they think the other team has bid too high, they might choose to bid just $1.)
- The team that bids closest to the actual value of the Showcase, without going over, wins the Showcase.
- The team that wins at least three of the five Showcases wins the event.

Option 1

If there are more than two teams, have each team guess the value of the Showcase in sequence.

Option 2

If you have a small group, play as pairs or individuals.

Debate: What difficult budget decisions must be made? (8 minutes)

In this event, the teams debate a controversial budget issue that has been discussed by the congregation in the past, or will be discussed in the near future.

- Give a brief description of the topic.
- Assign each team to a side.
- Give each team one minute to prepare an argument in favour of their position and one minute to present their argument.
- After the arguments have been presented, give each team 30 seconds to respond to the argument of the opposing side.
- Award points based on the number of team members involved in presenting the argument and how persuasively they made their case.

Example issue for debate:

The church has a surplus. We have received more money than we spent this year. What should we do with the extra money? Should we give the money away to a worthy cause or save the money for a future time of need?

Other possibilities include: addressing a deficit, a possible building project or significant capital investment, the use of bequeathed funds, giving to charitable causes

Option 1

With more than two teams, choose an issue with more than two perspectives.

Option 2

With four teams, consider doing two different debates and then have two teams face off in a final round on a different topic.

Option 3

If you have fewer than four people in your group, simply discuss the topic.

Pictogram: Why is it important to spend money in this way? (8 minutes)

Give each team a large sheet of paper, markers, and a copy of the church budget.

- Give each team 4 minutes to draw a pictogram (representative picture) describing why it is important to spend money on the items in the church budget, or what would happen if we did not.
- Give each team 1 minute to explain their image to a judge. The team with the most accurate and insightful pictogram wins the event.

Option

With a small group, make one or more pictures, and invite discussion.

Tiebreaker

For a simple tiebreaker, have each team write down the names of as many members of the church council, church board, elders group, or other financial decision-making body as they can in one minute.

Reflection and prayer: Budgeting our time (5 minutes)

Gather around the visual focus and connect the discussion to the reflection.

Teaching moment: We budget our time, as well as our money. We decide how much time we want to spend doing different things. It is important to budget time to spend with God, by going to church and setting aside personal time at home. We will spend the next three or four minutes thinking about how we budget our time or just thinking about God and feeling God's presence.

Ask each youth to find a personal space in the room. Ask the group to pray about their time and how they can "budget" it. Start the quiet reflection with the distinctive sound. Play music during this time.

Personal Giving

Module focus

What can we give besides money? What are the benefits of giving? What excuses do we use for not giving? How can we make the offering a meaningful time in the service? This module explores personal giving on both general and individual levels. It also addresses the use of the offering time during the worship service.

Leader preparation

Materials

- Chalkboard and chalk
- Chart paper and markers
- Copy of the handout (*My Offering*, p. 153) for each participant
- Pens/pencils
- Offering plate/bag/basket
- Visual focus and sound maker*
- Music player and music

Tasks

- *Discussion*
  —Arrange tables, chairs, and chalkboard according to the directions given in the section. Bring chart paper and markers for each table.
- *Reflection*
  —Choose music to accompany the reflection. Suggestions: "May the words I speak"—Bryan Moyer Suderman; "To be content"—Bryan Moyer Suderman; "Blessed be your name"—Matt Redman; "Let the River Flow"—Darrell Evans, 1995.

---

* See page 6 in the introduction for the suggested use of a distinctive sound and visual focus or worship centre for your *Reflection and prayer* time.

Session

Opening activity: Centipede (10 minutes)

Form a circle, and turn so that each person's right leg is on the inside of the circle.

- Take a large step toward the centre of the circle, so the group is tightly packed and the circle is round.
- Have everyone put their hands on the shoulders of the person in front of them
- Have everyone sit down at the same time.
- Try to walk, while remaining in the circle.

Option

If the group arrives gradually, and you want to start before everyone arrives, play Back to Back instead. Have a pair sit on the floor, back to back, with knees bent and elbows linked. On the count of three, the pair tries to stand up. Have the rest of the group join as they arrive, so the whole group can stand up at the same time. If time allows, use both games.

Teaching moment: Just as we all have an equal and important role to play in making these games work, we all have equal and important gifts to give to God and the church.

Discussion: Communal conversation on personal giving (25 minutes)

Rotating discussion groups are recommended for this conversation. Arrange tables and chairs so there is an outer ring of chairs and an inner ring of chairs, with tables in between, each seating 3 to 4 youth.

Place a piece of chart paper and markers on each table. Divide each paper into four numbered sections. Give the groups 4 to 5 minutes to discuss each question (see list below).

Gather the results of the small groups verbally or on a board. After each question, ask the youth sitting in the inner circle to rotate two or three chairs, so a different combination of youth is discussing each question.

Discussion questions

1. What can people give to God and the church besides money? Draw a tree diagram to illustrate your response. (For example, a large branch for job skills could lead to smaller branches for building, accounting, and teaching. The teaching branch could sprout branches for teaching Sunday school, practicing English with a refugee family supported by the congregation, coaching a children's soccer team, and preaching).
2. What are the benefits of giving to God and the church? List everyone who benefits from giving and the specific ways they benefit. (For example, the benefits to the specific giver and receiver, the church community, local community, and global community).
3. Money is also an important gift we can give to God and the church. What reasons do people give for spending money on themselves instead of others? Write down your ideas as questions or statements. (Example: I have to save for the future, so why should I make sacrifices when no one else my age does?)
4. How can we make the offering a meaningful time in the service? What can we do or think about during the offering to give ourselves to God, others, and the church? List ideas.

Reflection and prayer: Individual reflection on personal giving (10 minutes)

Place a container usually used to receive offering beside the visual focus. Gather around the visual focus and explain the time of reflection.

Distribute the handout and pens or pencils. Ask the youth to find a personal space in the room to reflect and record more personal answers to the questions you discussed as a group. Start the reflection time with the distinctive sound, and play music quietly.

Have the youth fold their papers and place them in the offering container. End the reflection time with the distinctive sound.

My Offering

1. What can I give to God and the church?

   _____
   _____

2. What benefits do I receive from the gifts I give?

   _____
   _____

3. How do I feel about the money I am giving to God right now? Do I make excuses for not giving? What are they?

   _____
   _____

4. What can I think about or do during the offering time of the service to give myself to God and the church?

   _____
   _____

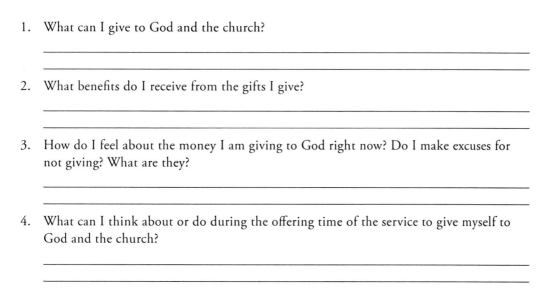

My Offering

1. What can I give to God and the church?

   _____
   _____

2. What benefits do I receive from the gifts I give?

   _____
   _____

3. How do I feel about the money I am giving to God right now? Do I make excuses for not giving? What are they?

   _____
   _____

4. What can I think about or do during the offering time of the service to give myself to God and the church?

   _____
   _____

Offering as Worship

Module focus

How can we lead the congregation in reflecting on the offering? This module creates space for preparing to lead the congregation in the offering portion of the worship service.

Leader preparation

Materials

- Paper
- Pens/pencils
- Sheets of paper from group discussions in Module 2 (p. 152)
- Worship resources
- Samples of offering invitations and prayers
- Copy of budget and pictograms from the budget game in Module 1 (p. 149)
- Visual focus and sound maker*
- Small pieces of paper (2 for each participant)
- Music player and music

Tasks

- *Discussion*
    —With the assistance of the worship planner, determine how the youth will contribute to the service, based on the four options described. Bring resources to assist the groups, based on how they will be involved.
- *Reflection and prayer*
    —Choose music on the theme. Suggestions: "One is the body"—*Sing the Journey* CD 1; "There are many gifts, but the same Spirit"—*HWB* 304; "If the Spirit of the Lord moves in my soul"—*Sing and Rejoice*
- Invite the planner of the service to join the group for this module.

---

* See page 6 in the introduction for the suggested use of a distinctive sound and visual focus or worship centre for your *Reflection and prayer* time.

Session

Opening activity: Prayer of dedication (2 minutes)

Giving God, Thank you for the many gifts, talents, and abilities you have given to us. We offer our talents and abilities to you and your church, as we prepare to lead in worship. Amen.

Preparing for worship: Planning to lead in the offering (33 minutes)

Divide the youth into planning groups of 3 to 6. Carefully consider the interests and abilities of the youth, as well as the worship context of your congregation, when selecting which elements to contribute to the offering. Worship leadership opportunities include:

1. Writing an invitation and prayer of dedication
Provide the group with:
*   The *Content for Teaching and Learning* for this unit (p. 144)
*   The large sheets of paper that resulted from the group discussions in Module 2
*   Examples of invitations and prayers used by worship leaders, or from a resource such as *Hymnal: A Worship Book*

Encourage creativity. If the group is having difficulty getting started, consider using an acrostic structure for the prayer, with a sentence attached to each letter of a phrase such as "God is good." Consider using a congregational response, such as "We offer our gifts to you, God," after each line read by a leader. Separate groups could also work on the invitation and dedication.

2. Choosing and sharing music for the reception of the offering
A group of youth musicians or an individual youth can prepare music to share during the offering. Encourage the planner(s) to think outside personal taste, and consider what music would help the congregation reflect on offering their gifts to God.

Consider providing a one-sentence introduction explaining the connection between the music selected and the offering.

3. Preparing a creative explanation of the budget
Hand out or point to the copy of the budget and the pictograms from the budget game in Module 1. Ask the group to develop a dramatic or visual presentation that explains how the offering is used and why it is important. Some ideas:
*   Make a slideshow presentation of images or photos to show during the receiving of the offering
*   Write a funny, yet appropriate and informative skit about the budget to share at an appropriate time during the service.

4. Considering the logistics of receiving the offering
A group of youth can work with an adult leader who usually coordinates the receiving of the offering, to learn how the process works. This group can also think about whether they wish to receive the offering according to the usual pattern, or try something different. Consider the creative suggestions found in the *Youth Service Suggestions* (p. 157).

Provide resources, support and encouragement to each group. Several minutes before the time of reflection, gather as a large group and ask the small groups to share the results of their labour and ensure the various elements form a unified whole.

Reflection and prayer: Identifying our gifts (10 minutes)

Each person present has contributed gifts in preparing to lead worship. It is important to take time to identify gifts in each other and ourselves. Gather around the visual focus and explain the time of reflection.

Give everyone a pencil and two small pieces of paper, and instruct them to write their names on both pieces. Have the youth return to their planning groups and exchange one of their papers with someone else.

Start the reflection time with the distinctive sound, and play the music you chose. On the paper with someone else's name, youth should write one gift the person contributed to preparing the offering. Then they should write one gift on their own paper. The gift can be broad (for example, listening to the ideas of others) or narrow, such as naming a specific sentence or word they contributed to a prayer.

Have youth return the papers to the people whose names are on them. Then ask everyone to place their own two papers around the visual focus. Thank God for the gifts God has given to the group and dedicating their worship leadership gifts to God.

Youth Worship Leadership Suggestions

Leading the offering

- Work with those who ordinarily coordinate the reception of the offering and subsequent handling of the money to ensure that all details are managed appropriately. Consider asking a youth or small group to work with an adult who regularly organizes the financial aspect of the offering, to learn about that part of the job.
- If an offering is not normally received in worship, consider developing a ritual in which the congregation can symbolically offer non-financial gifts. See the suggestions below.

Getting creative

Connecting to the service theme/season

- Use the offering invitation to connect the theme of the service or church season to the offering of our resources to God.
- Collect an additional cash offering to support a theme connected to the service, or in response to sharing on a topic such as homelessness, education, or AIDS.
- Use different offering containers for different seasons or themes:
  - —Treasure boxes during Epiphany
  - —Gift-wrapped boxes during Advent and Epiphany
  - —Large purses for a stewardship focus
  - —Soup bowls or grocery bags for a focus on hunger
  - —Bushel baskets at harvest time
  - —Flower pots in the spring
  - —A money tree made by attaching offering envelopes to a large plant
  - —A vessel connected to the work of members of the congregation, such as a hard hat, laptop case, "inbox," or tool box
  - —Baskets, bowls, and bags from around the world on World Communion Sunday or Mennonite World Conference Sunday

Offering the gifts of the youth

- The offering is often a moment in the service where specific gifts of the youth can be offered to God. Consider asking several youth to prepare and share a dance, create a slideshow of visual art made by artists or photographers in the group, or share their musical talents. Make sure they are leading the congregation in worship, not just performing.
- Consider asking each youth to symbolically offer one of their gifts to God with a symbolic object and one-sentence explanation while the offering is collected. For example, athletic ability could be symbolized by sports equipment or shoes, academic gifts with report cards, and friendship with photos or other symbols. Members of the congregation could also be invited the previous week to bring symbolic items to offer.

Offering more than money, or money that is more

- Take time during the offering to say thank you to God and to the congregation for the many gifts they offer, including time and service. Consider asking various groups to stand, but make sure no one feels excluded.
- Offer non-financial gifts. Take a moment during the offering to write:
  —Pledges of time or volunteer service
  —Words of encouragement to one another
  —Get-well notes to a church member
- Circulate volunteer sign-up sheets during the offering and dedicate them with the financial offerings.
- Dedicate church officers or a list of volunteers along with the offering at the beginning of each year, term, or quarter.
- Collect a small change offering in coffee cups to symbolize giving coffee money to a specified project.
- Ask each person to choose the bill or coin from their wallet that is in the best or newest condition, to show that we bring our first and best to God. Pass out paper, so people who do not have money can write or draw something that is their best.
- Invite members of the congregation who farm, garden, or bake to bring produce to the front during the offering to share. After the service, those who do not farm, garden, or bake can choose from the offering. Any extra can be given to a food bank.

Youth worship leadership checklist: Offering

Spiritual

1. Do the youth have the opportunity to pray together before the service?
2. Is the offering a meaningful moment and celebrative time of giving to God?
3. Is God's generosity named as the source of our giving?
4. Are the gifts received dedicated to God?
5. Is the offering integrated with the theme or scripture of the service?
6. Do the youth have the opportunity to celebrate and evaluate the service several days later?

Logistical

1. Are the basic necessities of offering collection organized, including who is receiving the offering and how the received funds taken care of?
2. Are clear instructions given as to how members of the congregation can participate?
3. Is the necessary technical equipment available and functional for the element prepared by each small group?
4. Are all participants aware of where they need to be and what they need to have with them at each point in time?
5. Does the offering flow smoothly out of and into the preceding and following elements?

The Lord's Supper

Unit focus

Through the Lord's Supper, the church remembers the life, death, and resurrection of Jesus and celebrates the community of faith as the body of Christ on earth. The Lord's Supper has been a central action of Christian worship since the New Testament Church. This unit explores the biblical foundations, contemporary interpretations, and personal significance of the Lord's Supper.

Many Mennonite churches limit participation in the Lord's Supper to baptized church members. This might restrict the leadership role of the youth as a group during the celebration of communion. In this unit, the youth bake bread for the Lord's Supper, rather than taking direct leadership during the service. Consider inviting baptized youth to participate more directly in the leadership of the service, or inviting the entire group to lead music, drama, or prayer relating to the Supper at other points during worship.

Unit outline

Content for Learning and Teaching
>   Biblical foundations for the Lord's Supper
>   Theological themes for the Lord's Supper
>   Resources

Curriculum Modules
>   Module 1: Introduction to the Lord's Supper
>   Module 2: Baking bread together

Youth Worship Leadership Suggestions
>   Leading the Lord's Supper
>   Getting creative
>   Youth worship leadership checklist

Content for Learning and Teaching

Biblical foundations for the Lord's Supper

We usually associate the Lord's Supper with the meal described in the synoptic gospels. In the Mennonite tradition, the foot washing narrative in the Gospel of John is also connected to the Lord's Supper. There are many other occasions where the gospels describe Jesus sharing meals with disciples, sinners, and crowds—a form of communion.

Theological themes for the Lord's Supper

Many theological themes are associated with the Lord's Supper. Central themes include:

- Giving thanks
- Remembering Jesus
- Feasting in the kingdom
- Sharing our lives and ourselves
- Reconciling and making peace
- The mystery of faith
- The presence of Christ
- Forgiveness
- Healing

- Christ's sacrifice and ours
- Christ's offering and ours
- Covenant
- Celebrating the victory of Christ
- Following Jesus
- Serving one another in the world
- Justice
- Community
- Christian unity

Quick rising bread recipe

Ingredients
1 cup warm water
¼ cup olive oil or salad oil
1 tsp sugar
2¼ cups flour (more for the counter)
1 tsp salt
1 package quick-rise instant yeast

Supplies
Large bowl
Small bowl
Measuring cups
Measuring spoons
Wooden spoon
Fork
Baking sheet
Grease or parchment paper for baking sheet

1. In a large mixing bowl combine:
    1 cup very warm, but not hot, water
    ¼ cup oil
    1 tsp sugar
2. In a small bowl combine:
    1 cup flour that has been stirred
    1 tsp salt
    Package of yeast
3. Add the flour mixture to the liquid mixture in the large bowl and beat well for 1 minute with a wooden spoon.
4. Add 1 more cup of flour and mix thoroughly. Incorporate about ¼ cup more flour, a small amount at a time, until dough is soft but not too sticky to knead.
5. Spread several tablespoons of flour on the counter. Place the dough on the floured counter and knead vigorously (press dough down with palm of the hand, fold over, and press again) about 3 minutes or 150 times, adding more flour as necessary to keep the dough from sticking to the counter.
6. Turn on the oven briefly, to just warm it up.
7. Grease a large baking sheet.
8. Divide dough into 3 pieces and shape each piece into a loaf. Place loaves several inches apart on the baking sheet. Prick all the way through each loaf with a fork, about six places in a row.
9. Turn off the oven. Place the cookie sheet with the loaves into the warmed oven and let the bread rise for 10 minutes.
10. Remove from oven. Preheat oven to 400 degrees Fahrenheit. (Bread will continue to rise on counter while oven preheats, about another 5 minutes.)
11. When oven is hot, bake loaves approximately 18 minutes or until tops are lightly browned and loaves sound hollow when tapped.

Resources

Confession of Faith in a Mennonite Perspective. Scottdale, PA: Herald Press, 1995.

"How to receive communion." *Mennonite Handbook.* Scottdale, PA: Herald Press, 2007.

Kreider, Eleanor. *Communion Shapes Character.* Scottdale, PA: Herald Press, 1997.

Rempel, John, ed. *Minister's Manual.* Scottdale, PA: Herald Press, 1998.

Weber Becker, Ann. *Faith for the Journey: Youth Explore the Confession of Faith.* Newton: Faith & Life Press, 1997.

Introduction to the Lord's Supper

Module focus

How have we experienced the Lord's Supper? What inspiration do we draw from the Bible in our celebration of the Lord's Supper? How do Mennonites understand the Lord's Supper? This module explores the nature and meaning of the Lord's Supper.

Leader preparation

Materials

- Fresh-baked bread
- Grape juice
- Cups and napkins
- Chalkboard and chalk *or* chart paper and markers
- Copy of the word scramble handout (p. 166) for each participant
- Copy of Lord's Supper section of *Confession of Faith in a Mennonite Perspective* for each participant (page 165)
- Bibles
- Paper
- Pens/pencils
- Visual focus and sound maker
- Music player, quiet instrumental music

Tasks

- *Opening activity*
  —Consider inviting several youth or adult leaders to share their experience of the Lord's Supper.
- *Discussion*
  —Write the questions for the first part of the discussion in a visible location.
- *Reflection and prayer*
  —Select an interesting visual focus that can contain diverse symbolic meanings. For example, use an unusual cross or candle, a lava lamp, abstract art or sculpture. The visual focus does not need to be explicitly Christian.

---

*   See page 6 in the introduction for the suggested use of a distinctive sound and visual focus or worship centre for your *Reflection and prayer* time.

Session

Opening activity: Snack and conversation (10 minutes)

Distribute fresh bread and grape juice and lead the entire group in an informal conversation about the Lord's Supper. Discuss the following:

- What do you remember about celebrations of the Lord's Supper in this congregation? Have you observed communion practices in other countries or churches?
- Is what we're doing right now communion? How is this snack the same as celebrating the Lord's Supper in church? How is it different?
- How do you experience the Lord's Supper, whether you're baptized or not? For example: Is it meaningful to watch? Frustrating to be excluded? Boring? Exciting to anticipate participating in the future? Invite the adult leaders or baptized youth to share about what receiving communion means to them.

Option

With a large group (16 or more), consider dividing into two groups, each with a separate adult leader to facilitate the conversation.

Teaching moment: The Lord's Supper, also called Communion or the Eucharist in some traditions, is not just eating and drinking bread and wine, although eating and drinking are an important part. It is about everything that surrounds the eating—words and actions, prayer, and the gathered community of faith. It is about experiencing and understanding the mystery of God and Jesus through something we can taste and touch and smell. Different Christian groups, including Mennonites, celebrate the Lord's Supper in different ways and understand what it means differently. However, the Lord's Supper is described in the Bible and is something almost all Christian groups practice.

Discussion: Biblical foundations (10 minutes)

Divide youth into groups of two or three and invite each group to read one of the texts and answer the questions.

- Last Supper in the synoptic Gospels: Mark 14:22-26, Matthew 26:26-30, Luke 22:15-20
- Last Supper in the Gospel of John: John 13:1-15
- Lord's Supper in Paul's Letter: 1 Corinthians 11:23-29
- Eating with tax collectors and sinners: Mark 2:15-17
- Feeding the 5,000: Matthew 14:15-21
- Manna in the wilderness: Exodus 16:10-17
- Recognizing the risen Lord: Luke 24:28-35
- Jesus as the Bread of Life: John 6:35, 41-51

Write the following questions in a visible location:

1. Who is present?
2. What happens?
3. What does God/Jesus do?
4. What does God/Jesus say?
5. How does this affect the meaning of communion?

Gather the entire group and invite small groups to share their responses to the questions.

Teaching moment: In celebrating communion, we bring all of these stories together. Communion has many meanings. When we share the Lord's Supper, we give thanks, remember Jesus, and celebrate that we are part of a community that includes Christians around the world. Mennonites understand communion in a certain way.

Discussion: A Mennonite understanding of the Lord's Supper (15 minutes)

Give each person the word scramble of *Handout 1* and the *Confession of Faith* statement of *Handout 2* (*The Lord's Supper*) and a pen or pencil. Encourage youth to work in pairs to complete the puzzle, using the *Confession of Faith* for clues. When most pairs are finished, go through the answers (key below). Ask the group to pick out themes that may be especially important for Mennonites. Try to incorporate these into the following teaching moment:

Teaching moment: Some of the most important themes of Mennonite understanding of the Christian life are: following Jesus (discipleship), community (attachment to a body of other believers—the church), and peace and reconciliation (a lifestyle that rejects violence, but seeks the good of all, including enemies). Note any other themes that emerge.

Take each theme in turn and ask the group how the Lord's Supper illustrates it. Ask how the theme is emphasized in your own communion services. Talk about particular practices in your congregation, and the youth's own experience of them, even if they are not baptized. For example, if people at your church break off small pieces from a large loaf—it may be more symbolic of unity than each person taking a cube of pre-cut bread. Or, while talking about "peace," your congregation may have a tradition of passing the peace before communion. The following may be helpful summaries:

Following Jesus: *We identify with Jesus in actually eating symbols of his body. We show that we want the life and teaching of Jesus to be central to who we are in the world.*

Community: *We share pieces of the same loaf and the same cup, reminding ourselves that together we make up the Body of Christ. We are committed to caring for each other and being accountable to one another.*

Peace: *Jesus' death on the cross is a symbol of forgiveness and sacrificial love, which is the opposite of revenge and violence. As we share the bread and the cup, we too adopt the way of forgiveness, non-violence, and service.*

Receiving communion reminds us of the commitment made at baptism, which covers all three of these areas: to follow Jesus, participate in supportive and accountable community, and be peace-makers.

Reflection and prayer: The power of symbols (10 minutes)

Gather around the visual focus.

Teaching moment: Symbols are powerful, because they can take on different meanings for different people at different times. Today we will use this object as a symbol for prayer.

Start the music and make the distinctive sound. Invite the youth to reflect for 2-3 minutes on how the visual focus is a symbol of prayer for them. (For example, the continual flow of a lava lamp may represent constant conversation with God, the soft light may represent the warm love of God experienced in prayer, or the tendency for beads of colour to get blocked at the top of the lamp may symbolize how sometimes it is difficult to pray.)

End with the distinctive sound, and invite the youth to share their reflections.

Answer key for the handout "The Lord's Supper in the Mennonite Church":

What we believe is happening

The Lord's Supper is a SIGN that represents Jesus' continued presence in our midst and helps us thankfully REMEMBER. At the Lord's Supper we renew our COVENANT with God and with each other. We remember and give THANKS for: God's acts of DELIVERANCE in the past and present, the FORGIVENESS of sins, and God's continuing GRACE in our lives. It is a JOYFUL yet SOLEMN event.

What we believe it means

Through the Lord's Supper, we recognize that we as a community are SUSTAINED by Jesus. We RECOMMIT ourselves to following Jesus. We recognize our UNITY with believers everywhere in all times and look forward to the feast in the KINGDOM of God that is to come.

How to prepare to participate

Those who have been BAPTIZED into the community, living at PEACE with God, RECONCILED with brothers and sisters in faith, and willing to be ACCOUNTABLE to the congregation, are invited to receive the bread and cup.

The Lord's Supper
in the Mennonite Church

Unscramble the words and fit them into the blanks. Use the description of the Lord's Supper in the *Confession of Faith in a Mennonite Perspective* to help if you get stuck.

GINS   DESTINSUA
MERMEREB   MITCOMREC
TENANCOV   TINYU
SKANTH   KMODING
LIVEACEREND   ZITDEPAB
SEVENGIORFS   CEEPA
CARGE   CONLEDIREC
LUFYOJ   TABLECCANUO
MOLESN

What we believe is happening

The Lord's Supper is a _ _ _ _ that represents Jesus' continued presence in our midst and

helps us thankfully _ _ _ _ _ _ _ _ . At the Lord's Supper we renew our

_ _ _ _ _ _ _ _ with God and with each other. We remember and give _ _ _ _ _ _

for: God's acts of _ _ _ _ _ _ _ _ _ _ _ in the past and present, the

_ _ _ _ _ _ _ _ _ _ _ of sins, and God's continuing _ _ _ _ _ in our lives. It is a

_ _ _ _ _ _ yet _ _ _ _ _ _ event.

What we believe it means

Through the Lord's Supper, we recognize that we as a community are _ _ _ _ _ _ _ _ _ _

by Jesus. We _ _ _ _ _ _ _ _ ourselves to following Jesus. We recognize our _ _ _ _ _ _

with believers everywhere in all times and look forward to the feast in the _ _ _ _ _ _ _

of God that is to come.

How to prepare to participate

Those who have been _ _ _ _ _ _ _ into the community, are living at _ _ _ _ _ _

with God, _ _ _ _ _ _ _ _ _ _ _ with brothers and sisters in faith, and willing to be

_ _ _ _ _ _ _ _ _ _ _ to the congregation are invited to receive the bread and cup.

The Lord's Supper

We believe that the Lord's Supper is a sign by which the church thankfully remembers the new covenant which Jesus established by his death. In this communion meal, the members of the church renew our covenant with God and with each other. As one body, we participate in the life of Jesus Christ given for the redemption of humankind. Thus we proclaim the Lord's death until he comes. (1)

The Lord's Supper points to Jesus Christ, whose body was given for us and whose shed blood established the new covenant. (2) In sharing the bread and cup, each believer remembers the death of Jesus and God's act of deliverance in raising Jesus from the dead. As we relive this event with a common meal, we give thanks for all God's acts of deliverance in the past and present, for the forgiveness of sins, and for God's continuing grace in our lives.

The supper re-presents the presence of the risen Christ in the church. As we partake of the communion of the bread and cup, the gathered body of believers shares in the body and blood of Christ (3) and recognizes again that its life is sustained by Christ, the bread of life.

Remembering how Jesus laid down his life for his friends, we his followers recommit ourselves to the way of the cross. Confessing our sins to one another and receiving forgiveness, we are to come as one body to the table of the Lord. There we renew our baptismal covenant with God and with each other and recognize our unity with all believers everywhere in all times.

All are invited to the Lord's table who have been baptized into the community of faith, are living at peace with God and with their brothers and sisters in the faith, and are willing to be accountable in their congregation.

Celebrating the Lord's Supper in this manner, the church looks forward in joy and hope to the feast of the redeemed with Christ in the age to come. (4)

1. 1 Corinthians 11:26.
2. Jeremiah 31:31-34; 1 Corinthians 11:24-25.
3. 1 Corinthians 10:16.
4. Luke 22:15-20, 28-30.

Baking Bread

Module focus

How can we contribute to the celebration of the Lord's Supper? During this module, youth bake communion bread.

Leader preparation

Materials

- Ingredients for chosen bread recipe
- Kitchen utensils
- Recipe cards
- Pens/pencils
- Visual focus and sound maker*
- Music player and music

Tasks

- *Opening activity*
  —Arrange chairs in a circle.
- *Discussion*
  —Speak to those who usually prepare the bread and cup for communion to determine how much bread is required and any other specifications.
  —Choose a bread recipe that will work with the communion style, time frame, kitchen facilities, and group size. Most bread needs time to rise. Some breads do not require as much rising time (one is included in the *Content for Learning and Teaching*, p. 159.)
  —Review the recipe and ensure you have enough ingredients and kitchen utensils. Secure the use of a kitchen, at church or in a home, with enough space for a number of small groups to bake together.
- *Reflection and prayer*
  —Choose appropriate music for reflection. Suggestions: "Be our guest"—from Beauty and the Beast, "Blessed be Your name"—Matt Redman
- Invite leaders normally involved in preparing the bread and cup to be present and assist with this module.

---

*   See page 6 in the introduction for the suggested use of a distinctive sound and visual focus or worship centre for your *Reflection and prayer* time.

Session

Opening activity: Food challenge (10 minutes)

Have youth sit in the circle of chairs as they arrive.

- Ask each person to hold their hands in front of them, fingers extended.
- Taking turns, moving around the circle, each person says a true food phrase. For example:

    I have eaten chocolate-covered ants.

    I have never been to McDonalds.

    I have eaten cat food.

    I have seen someone eat a fish eye.

    I have eaten 12 doughnuts in eight hours.

- If others can truthfully say the phrase, they fold down one finger. If the speaker is the only one who can truthfully say the phrase, he or she folds down a finger.
- The first person to fold down all 10 fingers wins.

Option

For a shorter game, play with five fingers.

Discussion: Baking bread together (25 minutes)

Bake communion bread together. With a larger group (and likely a larger congregation), divide into small groups to make multiple batches. Ensure each group has adequate supplies, equipment, and supervision. Depending on the timing of the module, the bread may be refrigerated or frozen until communion.

Option

If you are unable to bake, bring in a selection of breads from around the world. The group can do a taste test and choose which type(s) to use for communion together. Consider preparing wheat-free or other allergy-conscious bread options.

Time of reflection and prayer: Recipes of thanksgiving (10 minutes)

Teaching moment: Communion is a time when we thank God for what God has done in the past and commit to working with God in the future.

Make recipes of thanksgiving. Give each person a 4 x 6 recipe card and pen or pencil. Give the following instructions:

- At the top of the card, write a favourite food.
- List the ingredients in the food below.
- Beside the ingredients, write things you are thankful for in life. For example:

    Chocolate Chip Cookies

    Butter—family and friends who keep life smooth and delicious

    Brown sugar—sweet music

    Eggs—growth, potential for the future, opportunities

    Vanilla—flavour added to life by fun people, like my brother Dan.

    Baking soda—rising early this morning to run

    Flour—the basics: food, shelter, clothes

    Chocolate chips—exciting surprises

Sound the distinctive sound and play the music you have chosen. Allow 5 minutes for the group to complete their recipes.

Gather the group back together, and give everyone the opportunity to share their favourite food and recipe for thanksgiving. Close with a brief prayer such as:

Creator God, you provide us with so much delicious food and so many other good things. Today we give thanks for the many gifts you have given us. We also remember those who go without. We pray for people who are hungry for food, friendship, and spirituality, and ask that you will be with them in their hunger and fill all their needs. Amen.

Youth Worship Leadership Suggestions

Leading the Lord's Supper

- Talk with the pastors and church leaders about participation in the Lord's Supper. Many churches have specific traditions concerning observation of the Lord's Supper.
- If the Lord's Supper is extended only to baptized church members and not all youth are baptized, consider finding alternative ways for them to be involved in the service (for example, music, prayer, drama or scripture reading, operating the sound system, collecting communion cups.)
- Consider how baptized youth can be involved in the celebration of communion itself, through serving, or even officiating alongside an adult leader.

Getting creative

- Invite one or several youth to provide music while the bread and cup are served.
- Bake the bread during the service, adding different ingredients symbolically at different points. Make sure you leave time for baking.
- Bake a type of bread related to the theme of the service—for example, from a certain region of the world or historical era.
- The Lord's Supper can be a celebration of God's reign as well as a solemn remembrance. Decorate the worship space for a party with balloons and streamers.

Youth worship leadership checklist: The Lord's Supper

Spiritual

1. Do the youth have the opportunity to pray together before the service?
2. Do the youth have the opportunity to celebrate and evaluate the service several days later?

Logistical

1. Is there enough bread?
2. How will the bread stay fresh until the service?
3. Does a whole loaf need to be set aside for the communion leader to break?
4. Will the bread be cut before the service? Will youth be involved in preparing the bread before the service? If so, do they know when and where they should be?
5. Will it be announced verbally or printed in the bulletin that the youth made the bread for the service?
6. Do you need wheat-free or other allergy-conscious alternatives?
7. Is it clear who is preparing the wine or juice?

Youth Worship Service Planning Guide

The following is a step-by-step plan for helping your youth group develop an entire worship service.

1. **Pray.** Expect God to be engaged in the process of preparing for worship. You are not alone. It is not all up to you.

2. **Consider how and when youth can be involved in the planning process** as you read through the following points. Take into account the age, size and commitment of your group. Consider distributing the *Gifts and Interests Survey* in Appendix 2 (p. 173). In most cases, adult leaders can develop a framework for the service (Steps 1-5) which the youth can adapt.

3. **Choose a date.** Communicate with congregational worship leaders and pastors. Avoid interrupting other worship series or seasons of the church year. Once a date is chosen, communicate it clearly to both youth and parents. Schedule rehearsal time and reserve rehearsal space.

4. **Choose a Scripture text and theme.** Ideally, work with familiar content from Sunday school or Bible Study. If not, devote at least one session to exploring the chosen Scripture text and theme together. Consider choosing a theme associated with the date, especially if it falls during a significant season of the Christian year.

5. **Create an order of worship.** Using a standard worship service in your congregation as a guide, list the elements that could be included in the service. This may include opening and closing words, Scripture, preaching, music, sharing time, prayer, offering collection and announcements among many other possibilities. Choose carefully which elements will be included in the youth service. Consider incorporating new or different elements. Give special attention to the flow between elements and the movement of mood, ideas, and worship leaders.

6. **Gather resources** for various elements of the service for youth or adult leaders to draw on in the planning process.

7. **Plan the details of the words, actions, ideas, and moods of the service.** Combining the following approaches:
   a. *Small group planning.* Carefully construct small groups based on the abilities and interests expressed by youth to address different parts of the service. For example, small groups could: 1) choose and lead music, 2) design and create visuals, 3) prepare and present words for worship leading, 4) prepare and present a time for children and short sermons, 5) plan and rehearse a dramatic Scripture presentation, and 6) write and lead a congregational prayer. Support each small group and ensure adequate communication between groups.

   Encourage small groups to involve people from outside their group as necessary—for example, in drama and music. Make sure each group has clear written instructions regarding what they are responsible for. For example, the visual group may be required to create a large dramatic visual, arrange a display at the front of the church, design a bulletin cover, or communicate with the music group if song lyrics are projected visually. Additional resources relating to elements of worship are included with each Unit in the Youth Worship Source Book.

    b. *Large group planning.* Consider whether certain elements, such as a drama with a large cast or a musical piece sung as a choir, would be better prepared and presented as a large group. Ensure adequate rehearsal time is allotted and there are ways for youth with diverse gifts to participate.

    c. *Individual planning.* Especially with a small youth group, consider ways individuals can be involved in preparing prayers or short sermons, or leading worship through sharing music or other gifts and talents. Encourage individuals to prepare and rehearse independently, yet ensure they receive adequate resources and support.

8. **Integrate and communicate.** Once all small groups and individuals have outlined their contributions, talk through the service together. Pay special attention to the flow of mood, ideas, and people in the transitions between elements. Does the service fit together as a whole? Is the central theme and Scripture text clear? Does each group and youth understand how their contributions fit into the whole?

9. **Check the details.** Speak with a pastor or worship leader to ensure all of the aspects associated with worship in your congregation are taken care of. For example, ensure individuals have been identified to serve as greeters, ushers, and sound technicians.

10. **Rehearse.**

    a. *Small group rehearsals.* Encourage and support each small group as they practice their contributions to the service.

    b. *Large group rehearsals.* Practice elements of the service that incorporate the entire group in the worship space.

    c. *Individual rehearsal.* Encourage individual contributors to rehearse independently.

11. **Run through the service** from start to finish in the worship space using the technical equipment. Make sure each contributor knows where they need to be, what they need to have with them, and what they are to be doing at each point during the service. If necessary, run through the service more than once.

12. **Pray** together before leading worship.

Suggestions for a strong service

- Make a simple but dramatic visual to capture the spiritual imagination of the congregation. Consider finding ways to reuse the visual on other occasions.
- End the service with all of the youth at the front of the church. See Unit 2 for ideas for sending words presented by a large group.
- Try something new or different that is meaningful for the youth. At the same time, avoid doing something new and different for each element of the service. Keep it simple.
- Remember to keep the focus of the service on God not the youth. The youth are worship leaders not performers.

Times and places for youth worship leadership

- Sunday morning worship in local congregations is the primary time and place for youth worship leadership.
- Take the youth service on the road to a senior's residence or Christian school.
- Encourage youth to take leadership in planning worship for a youth retreat or service trip.
- Plan a special additional seasonal service with the youth. For example, lead worship for Maundy Thursday, Good Friday, Advent, Pentecost, the church picnic, or a commissioning or celebration service.

Worship Leadership Gifts Survey

What is your name? _____

What languages do you speak? _____

		Have you been involved in:	Would you be interested in:	
		Yes	Yes	Maybe
Participating	Attending Worship			
Speaking	Worship leading alone			
	Worship leading with a group			
	Reading scripture			
	Making announcements			
Music	Choosing music			
	Singing a solo			
	Singing with a group			
	Playing an instrument (instrument(s):_____)			
	Writing lyrics			
	Composing music			
Prayer	Writing a prayer			
	Reading a prayer			
	Leading a spontaneous prayer			
Visuals	Making a banner			
	Designing a bulletin cover			
	Creating a visual display			
	Compiling a slideshow			
	Filming a video			
Drama	Acting in a drama			
	Writing a drama			
	Directing a drama			
Preaching	Preparing or presenting a message for children			
	Preaching alone			
	Preaching with a partner or group			

Dance	Dancing alone (type(s):_____)			
	Dancing with a group (type(s):_____)			
	Choreographing dance (type(s):_____)			
Ushering	Greeting			
	Receiving the offering			
Food	Baking			
Technology	Operating sound equipment			
	Operating visual equipment			
Other	(Expand:_____)			

Acknowledgments

Special thanks to:

Everyone involved in the Logos program at First Mennonite Church, Kitchener—especially the youth! Thanks also to adult leaders including: Sarah Pinnell, Peter Jutzi, David Neufeld, Peggy Roth, and Aaron Woolner.

All who knowingly and unknowingly contributed to the source book: Delphine Bauman, Mary Louise Bringle, many chapel leaders at Conrad Grebel University College, Ken Hull, Rebecca Janzen, Arlene Kehl, Marlene Kropf, Heather Mann, Nancy Mann, Joél Schmidt, Mike Turman, and Maegan Wagler.

David Johnson, Susan Johnson, Daniel Johnson and Michael Koop who listened and responded to many ideas and made dozens of helpful suggestions.

Jeff Steckley at Mennonite Church Eastern Canada and Ed Janzen at Conrad Grebel University College for their support of the project.

Byron Rempel-Burkholder, Eleanor Snyder, Mary Meyer, Karen Jantzi, and Mennonite Publishing Network for valuable editorial advice and for making a vision a reality.

—Sarah Kathleen Johnson, June 2009

Printed in the United States
221411BV00003B/1/P